# INDIA'S FOREIGN POLICY

*Towards Resurgence*

# INDIA'S FOREIGN POLICY

*Towards Resurgence*

*Editor*

Dhruv C Katoch

INDIA FOUNDATION
Analysis • Advocacy • Awareness

PENTAGON PRESS LLP

INDIA'S FOREIGN POLICY: **Towards Resurgence**
*Editor: Dhruv C Katoch*

First Published in 2019



ISBN 978-93-86618-78-8





*Published by*
PENTAGON PRESS LLP
206, Peacock Lane, Shahpur Jat
New Delhi-110049
Phones: 011-64706243, 26491568
Telefax: 011-26490600
email: rajan@pentagonpress.in
website: www.pentagonpress.in

Printed at Aegean Offset Printers, Greater Noida, U.P.

# Contents

## ECONOMY AND SOFT POWER



## NEIGHBOURS AND THE NEIGHBOURHOOD

# Introduction

*Dhruv C Katoch*

In February 2018, India Foundation held a workshop on India's foreign policy—perhaps the first of its kind—to enable a better understanding of the subject for Indian and foreign nationals interested in the subject. Large segments of the public across the world remain blissfully ignorant of the foreign policy of their respective countries, believing it to be something which is solely in the domain of the government. Yet, foreign policy effects the people in a direct way. It has an impact on the national economy, on consumption patterns, energy needs, defence and practically every aspect of the life of the people. Its primary role is the maintenance and preservation of National Interest, hence how a nation conceives its national interest and seeks to protect and promote it through its foreign policy must be a matter of public importance and discourse.

Not many people are aware that perhaps the first treatise on statecraft was crafted by an Indian. Chanakya's Arthashastra, written in the fourth century BCE, in the reign of Chandragupta Maurya and later his son Bindusara, remains the first definitive work laid out for managing a nations' foreign and domestic affairs in clear and precise terms. The treatise remained an influential piece of work right up to the 12th century CE, but thereafter, tragically, this epic treatise on statecraft, economic policy and military strategy, was lost to the world till it was rediscovered in 1905 by R. Shamasastry, and published in 1909. The first English translation was published in 1919, from the original Sanskrit.

The Chinese general and military strategist, Sun Tzu predated Chanakya by about a hundred years, and is credited as the author of *The Art of War*, an influential work of military strategy, which continues to influence many competitive endeavours in the world. In Europe, it was Machiavelli (1469–

1527 CE), an Italian diplomat, politician and poet of the Renaissance period, who is often called the father of modern political science. Later, it was Carl von Clausewitz, a Prussian general and military theorist who laid stress on the moral and political aspects of war. All these writings have had an impact on the foreign policies of nations across the world, in greater or lesser measure, depending on their respective cultural proclivities.

India's past continues to reverberate in its foreign policy today. Ancient India had contacts with places as far out as Rome and Greece to the West and China to the East, but the statecraft followed was not expansionist, a notable exception being the Chola Empire (300 BCE-1279 CE). This remains a constant in India's foreign policy, which retains a level of idealism, realism and independence of action.

The values which India believes in have for millennia, been a part of its cultural heritage. Justice, equality, liberty, equal opportunities for all, friendship with our neighbours, peaceful resolution of disputes and other aspects have always been part of the Indian ethos. Today, India is a rising power and constitutes "...one of the most fascinating and important stories of the past two decades, symbolising, along with China, the fundamental shift of power towards Asia.... The need to understand India's perspective has never been greater, and today no global challenge—be it climate change, nuclear proliferation or poverty reduction—can be tackled successfully without India's active contribution and engagement."[1]

How will a rising India interact with the rest of the world? What will be the impact of its cultural influence? What role does it seek to play in addressing the challenges of the day, such as climate change, poverty reduction and terrorism? It was to enable an understanding of India's foreign policy that Shri Ram Madhav, National General Secretary of the Bharatiya Janata Party (BJP), and Member, Board of Governors, India Foundation, conceptualised the first workshop in February 2018 on India's foreign policy. The leading thinkers and practitioners of the subject—India's External Affairs Minister, Ministers of State in the Ministry of External Affairs (MEA), the Foreign Secretary and other secretaries in the MEA, former and serving ambassadors, and specialists in the subject were invited to give their views on the subject and on the path India's foreign policy has taken since independence in 1947. This book is a collation of the talks delivered in the workshop. The recordings were painstakingly transcribed by Ms Shreya Challagalla, Research Fellow, India Foundation. In the process of editing this book, if any errors have crept in, the responsibility is that of the editor alone and not on the distinguished individuals who spoke at the workshop. It is my hope and belief that the book will be a useful source material for those who desire to understand the intricacies of India's foreign policy.

Jai Hind.

## NOTE

[1]Stuenkel, Oliver. (2013). Emerging India: A Farewell to Multilateralism? *Indian Foreign Affairs Journal*, 8, 413–427.

# India's Foreign Policy: An Overview

*Sushma Swaraj*

The various facets of India's foreign policy include our major bilateral relations, our approach to multilateral diplomacy, our strategic and security priorities and our soft power outreach initiatives, among others. Soon after forming the Government at the Centre, the BJP-led NDA government sent out a strong signal that its approach to foreign policy issues would be one that befits the rising global nature of India—an innovative, confident, bold and pragmatic approach that welcomes one and all to share our growth. In the last three and half years, this government has explored new approaches and charted new directions on visualisation and implementation and a new visibility and energy in our foreign policy has been noticed all around the world. Towards this end, right from the very beginning, all leaders of the neighbouring countries were invited for the swearing-in ceremony of Prime Minister Narendra Modi and his cabinet, and on 26 January 2018 all ten heads of ASEAN nations were invited as Chief Guests for our Republic Day parade. This indicates India's strong commitment to regional priorities.

It has been rightly said that, '*Samman, Samvad, Samriddhi, Suraksha, Sanskriti evam sabyatha*' are the driving forces behind India's global engagement. There is today a greater expectation of India's role in the world, as reflected by India emerging as a natural participant in several regional and global discourses. Our constructive approach to global issues was widely recognised recently during our entry into the Wassenar Arrangement, Australia Group, our membership of the SCO and the initiation of the International Solar Alliance (ISA). The primary driver of this change has been the nature of domestic political evolution that India experienced in 2014. For the first time in nearly three decades, the people of India brought into power a Central Government with decisive majority in the Lower House of the Parliament, voting for change and good governance. It was also a call reflective of aspirations of India's youth. The government has responded to the mandate by unveiling a range of measures and initiatives to aid the economic transformation of India. All this conveyed a message that India is a country with a decisive and energetic leadership, and a government which is committed to transformative change.

Another development, not unrelated to the first, is the way the world has begun to look at India. In the last two years, the India story has revived itself, because of the energy and rigour demonstrated by the Government. India has emerged as the fastest growing major economy in the world. Even in the face of difficult global economic climate, relevant agencies have rated India as an investment destination and there has been a nearly 40 per cent surge in inward Foreign Direct Investment (FDI). There has also been a remarkable increase in India's position on the Ease of Doing Business index. There's a clear sense of recalibration in our foreign policy to take advantage of these developments and to strengthen them through proactive and energetic diplomacy.

In terms of our international economic outreach, there has been an unprecedented outreach of India's diplomatic canvas at the highest levels—both in terms of regularity and quality of engagements, even as we are engaged with our traditional partners with greater warmth and frequency. The coverage of our diplomacy has extended to new countries and regions and to those countries that have not received adequate attention for a long time—West and Central Asia, our immediate neighbourhood and the Indo-Pacific region. On 23 January 2018, in his address at the World Economic Forum's Annual Meeting 2018 in Davos, Switzerland, Prime Minister Narendra Modi spoke of India's vision to create a shared future, in an increasingly divided and fractured world. Improving connectivity and promoting freer movement of goods, ideas and culture is a crucial part of this mission. Whether it is domestic, external or regional, in the decades to come, connectivity will determine how India and Asia achieve levels of growth, employment and prosperity. There is now growing awareness that lack of physical and digital infrastructure, both within India and the larger South Asian neighbourhood and beyond, is the major constraint in both our capability and competitiveness. However, the connectivity initiatives must be based on internationally accepted norms, good governance, rules of law, on terms of transparency and equality. It must be done in a manner that respects sovereignty and territorial integrity.

In the past year, there has been significant progress in terms of infrastructure connectivity projects undertaken by India in our neighbourhood—rail, road, ports, inland waterways, shipping, energy and fuel transmission are being implemented with our partners in the neighbourhood to recognise the goal of a secure, prosperous and economically connected South Asia. Multi-nodal projects are underway in Bangladesh and Myanmar, with an aim of eliminating the physical connectivity gap between South Asia and the ASEAN region, giving impetus to our 'Act East' Policy. We are working with our international partners to further develop this into an Asia-Africa Growth Corridor, which will revitalise the country's old linkages of trade, commerce and connectivity between the two largest continents of the world.

In the West, we saw the inauguration of the first phase of the Chabahar port in 2017, with the inaugural consignment of Indian wheat delivered to Afghanistan through Chabahar and the establishment of the India-Afghanistan airfield corridor. These innovative initiatives, along with our engagement with partners in Central Asia, the international North-South transportation corridor, paved the way for the operationalisation of the Chabahar port, helping develop an alternate, robust route to promote trade and transit with Afghanistan and the wider region.

In the historic launch of the South Asia satellite, we demonstrated our commitment to sharing the benefits of our technological capabilities with our regional partners. As a first responder in terms of emergencies and natural disasters, our proactive and professional approach in providing humanitarian assistance and disaster relief (HADR) has underlined India's readiness to stand by its friends in times of need, be it the safe evacuation of civilians in conflict zones, rendering earthquake and flood relief in Nepal and Sri Lanka or delivering fresh water to the Maldives or providing humanitarian assistance to displaced persons in Bangladesh. The ASEAN-India Commemorative Summit and our Chairmanship of BRICS in October 2016 at Goa held in conjunction with the BRICS-BIMSTEC outreach, both were a resounding success for our diplomacy. This was followed by the 'Heart of Asia' Summit which affirmed India's commitment to partnering with Afghanistan in its transition. In 2015, the India-Africa Forum Summit (IAFS), with the participation of 54 African countries unveiled our dynamic and transformative agenda of resurgence between India and the nations of Africa. IAFS itself was preceded by two landmark summits with specific island nations in the Pacific region. These events were a testimony to our outreach to smaller nations and our willingness to build a new paradigm of South-South cooperation. India's outreach to Central Asia has seen great progress with the Prime Minister visiting the region several times, with the latest being Kazakhstan for the 17th SCO Summit in June 2017, where India was admitted as a full-member of the SCO.

Counter-terrorism has emerged as a crucial area of cooperation with the countries in the Central Asian region. Central Asia is also one of the largest beneficiaries of Indian technical and economic assistance. The steady growth of our relations with the US has been a matter of great satisfaction, as much as the conformation of our traditional partnership with Russia, France, the UK and the EU. Our partnership with countries like Japan and Germany have been reenergised, with a focus of leveraging these partnerships for our domestic economic transformation. For a developing country like India, diplomacy must be used to enable domestic growth. Never has this principle been more salient than the working of diplomacy now. In the past three and a half years, advancement of India's commercial interest has been at the forefront of all Indian diplomatic activity. These efforts have hugely been facilitated by the enunciation of concrete domestic objectives identified by the government under its flagship programs. This has enabled Indian diplomacy to serve the international landscape and best identify institutional partners that can contribute to projects like 'Make in India,' 'Skill India,' 'Digital India,' 'Smart Cities,' 'Swachh Bharat,' etc.

Another important focus area of the government has been to rekindle and strengthen our linkages with the diaspora, as shown by the enthusiastic participation in the first ever Person of Indian Origin (PIO) Parliamentarians earlier this month. Many of these children of India have risen to positions of importance in their chosen professions, who contribute materially to advance India's relations with their host nations. Some of them are equally keen to contribute directly to India's social and economic development, through their investment, skills and experience. I can say with confidence that this government has finally put Indians back at the heart of India's foreign policy—whether it is through increased resources or focus on protection facilitation of the large community of Indian nationals who live and work abroad or through transforming the public interface of the Ministry of External Affairs. As I have said on previous occasions, my ministry now takes pride in being the 'madatkaar' ministry. The passport offices in India and the consular departments of our missions and posts abroad are the visible face of the Ministry as seen by our citizens, transformed through the use of digital platforms and innovative use of social media. We are also placing emphasis on creating robust emergency response systems in parts of the world where there is a large concentration of Indian citizens, to protect them in times of crisis.

The above are just some of the key aspects of India's revitalised foreign policy over the last three and a half years. I am sanguine that we will continue to focus our capabilities in furthering the global aspirations of our country.

# THE SHAPING OF INDIA'S FOREIGN POLICY

# 1

# The Shadow of History on Foreign Policy

*M. J. Akbar*

History illuminates, of course; but it also intrigues, provoking questions that do not permit easy answers. Francis Fukuyama famously identified the end of history only to discover that history is like the ghost that never sleeps, a sceptre that can suddenly burgeon into terrifying dimensions just when we were all drifting towards that comfort zone called complacence.

For much of the contemporary world, history was born a hundred years ago. The end of the first world war, and the collapse of three empires, marked the onset of a new order that culminated at the end of the second world war in the wreck of colonialism. The nation state, its sovereignty defined by the will of the people rather than the sword of a monarch, emerged as the building block of the redesigned architecture of international stability. In 1918, there were about 55 political entities on the globe; today there are nearly 200 members of the United Nations.

Nationalism could not be suppressed even where the past continued to linger through reinvention, as in the Soviet Union, or in the less structured regions of "Western influence." By the last two decades of the 20th century, neo-colonisation was being challenged, with various degrees of success, across Asia, Africa, Central Europe and Latin America. In a striking development, sovereign states either slipped out, or crashed out, of superpower blocs to strengthen their integrity and reshape their economic future through new and compatible regional alliances of their choice. The 21st century will be an era of alliances or formations like ASEAN, BIMSTEC, European Union (EU),

African Union, BRICS and Arab League, co-operation structured on compatibility and mutual confidence. It goes without saying that all such formations will not enjoy the same success, but this is the pattern that has already gathered momentum.

It is not widely known that before the charter of the United Nations, conquest of countries was perfectly legal. The British Empire may have been immoral, but it was not illegal. One consequence of the end of domain or domination over land, which did not become immediately obvious, is gathering pace as the present century matures. Denied acquisition of land, the major and aspirant powers are gradually shifting the competition for zones of dominance on water. Water has no boundaries. It has become what land was in the 19th century and earlier.

Seas have been the principal highways for trade and supplementary avenues for military adventurism and conquest. Trade continues to find its way through water. But we are going to see a significant escalation in the new great game, for the blue map of the world is also a treasure-house of natural resources. The growing recognition of a nomenclature, Indo-Pacific, signals the arrival of India as a consequential presence on the blue map. The difference is that India seeks freedom of navigation, rather than competition or conflict, in consonance with a fundamental tenet of its foreign policy philosophy.

India has learnt lessons from the traumas of its past. We became vulnerable to colonisation not because Europeans were strong, but because we had become weak. Foreign traders and armies came because they were attracted by our agricultural and manufacturing wealth. No one seeks to conquer a poor region; no one was interested in the deserts of Iran and Arabia until black gold was discovered beneath its surface. Till the 19th century, India and China accounted for half of the world's manufacturing output. We were taught the abrasive nuances of gunboat diplomacy, and the menace of economic aggression, with artificially priced trade and debt as its battering rams. Colonial power also grew out of the barrel of a gun, but we learnt that guns which sustain foreign domination can also be purchased with the wealth of the conquered. Britain made India pay for its own defeat. We discovered that our geographic vulnerability was not restricted to traditional routes used by invaders from central Asia; Portugal, France and Britain came by seas to our west, south and east. The Hooghly river was as vulnerable as the Khyber pass. These lessons have to be absorbed into foreign policy, for freedom is not always synonymous with independence.

The age of European colonisation began in India and ended in India. Till Mahatma Gandhi took up the challenge, the British Raj seemed invincible. When Gandhi launched his first mass movement, in 1919 and 1920, an Indian member of the Viceroy's Council famously wondered what this man in a dhoti thought he was doing; the British Empire would last 400 years. That was conventional wisdom. After Gandhi, the British Raj could not last for three decades. Remarkably, Gandhi punctured the greatest empire in history with an Indian idea, Satyagraha, the power of justice and truth riding on a non-violent mass uprising. The emergence of India as a sovereign nation state that was both free and independent changed the strategic narrative of the world.

But colonisation still had the wile in its last phase, the 1940s, to claim a last laugh. The price of India's independence was partition, which created a country in the name of religion, and within ten weeks of inception triggered the first "Jihad" after the second world war by invading the princely state of Jammu and Kashmir. In October 1947, Pakistan sought through war what would have been negotiated across the table, setting off a conflict that has not ended. It is an interesting fact that, in the last hundred years, no one who has started a war of conquest has won it. Undaunted by repeated failure, Pakistan shifted in the 1980s to a strategy of "war by other means". This was disguised terminology for terrorism. Occasional war became the vicious cycle of permanent war.

There is a second dimension. In 1792, Revolutionary France declared war against Austria and Prussia, its generals marked a turning point in history by urging troops to fight in the name of France, rather than in the name of the King. Today, the Indian army fights in the name of the Republic. Pakistan's army fights in the name of Allah.

India's most persistent security threat comes from a birth defect. The conflict with Pakistan is not just geographical; it is ideological. It is about whether a contemporary nation shall be a democracy or a theocracy. It is a debate about whether a nation shall reflect the unity of a geo-cultural ethos, or whether the Indian subcontinent should be balkanised. India chose to be a modern democracy.

It was axiomatic, after 1947, that a post-colonial, democratic India should seek to restructure the inherited framework of security policy. But our first efforts, through the 1950s, were a mixture of idealism and naiveté. Prime Minister Jawahar Lal Nehru thought that the desire for peace was equivalent to peace, an approach that inevitably became an invitation to invasion by a neighbour with whom we shared contentious borders. Prime Minister Nehru embraced the world stage with a non-aligned clasp that was a useful finesse around the dangerous Cold War, but faltered badly when applied to India's immediate security interests. He appointed a quasi-socialist defence minister, V.K. Krishna Menon, who actually sought to downgrade defence production. Nehru's biggest foreign policy investment, an entente with China, ended in Indian humiliation during the 1962 border war.

There is an old Sufi saying: What do you do when you are trapped in a vicious circle? Draw a bigger circle. India and China have, thus far, discovered the virtues of the larger circle. The relationship between India and China, particularly over the last five years, is an object lesson in how the space and opportunities of the larger circle can obviate the tensions of a smaller circle. They rose above the boundary dispute, and found mutual reward in more productive engagement. This did not eliminate tension; but it did provide a mechanism for defusing it.

The confrontation over Doklam could have risen on a self-perpetuating axis to a point of no control. If Beijing was testing Prime Minister Narendra Modi's resolve, or his leadership, or his ability to manage a crisis without tremor, or the capacity of India's armed forces to hold their ground, then it must have got a clear read-out of all answers. Once the temperature came down, India and China returned to the more important business of finding a compatible way forward. Our policy is mature: keep differences from becoming disputes, and prevent disputes from becoming conflicts. There is always a way forward through a dialogue. Security management can stop short of war. War is a waste of resources which are needed for the prime challenge of poverty elimination and egalitarian welfare.

The two cardinal purposes of governance are surely prosperity for the people and security for the nation. The two are joined at the hip. One is not possible without the other. Both have internal and external dimensions. Today, a nation's economy cannot afford to remain insular; insularity breeds stagnation if not regression. India's present foreign policy is a pursuit of these complementary objectives.

Under Prime Minister Modi, security is a comprehensive focus on impregnable defence of the nation and projection of its interests. When India speaks of its defence forces, it means what it says; it does not believe in offence. India understands the meaning of defence: every inch of Indian soil shall be protected, and the loss of any Indian life will demand accountability.

The world now recognises that India is not interventionist, does not destabilise, and believes that we live in a time of nation states that are equal, with equal rights and responsibilities. Countries have different capacities, but the way ahead is to search for economic and strategic harmony to ensure peace. It is this credibility that has enabled India to maintain excellent relations across binaries. There is no better example than India's equation with Israel and Palestine. Prime Minister Modi began 1918 with a hugely successful week-long visit by Israeli Prime Minister Benjamin Netanyahu. The next event on the diplomatic calendar was opening the Davos conference. He returned home to host the heads of state or government of all ASEAN states as guests for India's Republic Day on 26 January. Immediately thereafter, he left for Palestine, stopping in Amman en route; he reached Ramallah on King Abdullah of Jordan's personal plane. Palestine honoured him with its highest award. His next stops were UAE and Oman. Meanwhile, in late January, foreign minister Sushma Swaraj visited Saudi Arabia, and in early March, Iran's foreign minister Javad Zarif came to Delhi.

The significance of the presence of every ASEAN head of state or government can hardly be underestimated. It was an assertion of the success of India's "Look East" policy, which has now evolved into an "Act East" programme. India and ASEAN are building an economic bridgehead which can become, if all goes well, an anchor of the world economy within the coming decade. This is the prosperity side of the foreign policy coin.

Simultaneously, India and Indonesia are repairing a relationship that had got lost in some void which neither side wanted, but, equally, which neither country did much to fill. That void is now being filled. January 2019 witnessed an important first, when a cargo ship from Aceh unloaded goods at Port Blair in the Andamans. The distance between the southern tip of Andamans and Aceh is not much more than a hundred nautical miles, but neither country had made any serious effort to bridge it. Indonesia at long last has become a neighbour of India.

Prime Minister Modi has, in a very short while, redefined the meaning of a neighbour. Reach is more important than geography. Proximity is of little use if you cannot reach your destination. Today, India's neighbourhood stretches from Indonesia in the east to the Gulf in the west. India's strategic philosophy is no longer limited to the perspective of a land south of the Himalayas; India is also a nation north of the ocean. India now plays a pivotal role in Asia. If it can continue its journey on the arc of an inclusive, egalitarian economy in the coming 10 years, and remain a bulwark of security and stability, it will play a decisive role in shaping the fate of Asia and thereby of the 21st century.

# 2

## Indian Strategic Thought

*Shakti Sinha*

Does India have a strategic thought? Or is it something that is being developed in its initial stages, particularly after the breakdown of the Nehruvian consensus that guided India since 1947? The first, and well-known study on this was made by George Tanham, who came to the conclusion that Indian political elites showed "little evidence of having thought coherently or systematically about national strategy" (Tanham 1992, 130). His reasoning was that the forces of history and culture in India had "worked against" the cultivation of a strategic mind-set (Tanham 1992, 130, 131).

In more recent times, Indian strategic thinker and scholar Bharat Karnad has argued that as India does not satisfy the ten criteria for "power-hood" identified by him, it cannot be called a great power. The criteria enunciated by Karnad are "driving vision, outward-thrusting nature backed by strong conviction and sense of national destiny and matching purpose, an inclination to establish distant presence and define national interests within the widest possible geographical ambit, the confidence to protect and further those interests with proactive foreign and military policies, the building up of meaningful conventional armed forces backed by a proven and tested thermonuclear arsenal, and a willingness to use coercion and force in support of national interests complemented by imaginative projection and use of both soft power and hard power to expansively mark its status in the external realm" (Karnad 2015, 1). All this would suggest that there is nothing called Indian strategic thinking, or at best that such thinking was in its early stages.

It is important to use history to further explore the existence or lack of Indian strategic thought. History is used to establish that India was never a country until the British Raj created one. Proponents of this thought include persons like John Strachey who famously said, "there is not and never was an India"[1] and Churchill, who went on to say, "India is as much of a country as the equator is" (Tharoor 1997, 1). Contemporary analysts too share this belief and strengthen their argument by citing India's amazing diversity, size and lack of political unity historically. However, "country" is probably a wrong word to begin with as it is identified with being a "nation-state". The term "nation" is better suited to describe the land. To measure India against the attributes of a "nation-state" is an unfair question, just like judging a horse by its abilities to climb a tree. Asking the right questions is important, just as categorisation is very important. The words "nation" and "nationalism" are keywords and in each case one should assess which came first. It is said that Italian nationalism created Italy, but the opposite is true for civilisational nations like China and India. Nationalism is a very modern concept; a nation on the other hand is shared consciousness and is embodied in beliefs, myths and symbols. A broadly defined territorial space is very important as without it, the concept of cultural unity is difficult to develop or sustain. From here we can derive concepts like home, kinship, family, mother and motherland.

The political scientist Anthony D. Smith in his book *Nationalism and Modernism: A Critical Survey of Recent Theories of Nations and Nationalism* makes the point that all nations today have four elements—community, territory, history and a sense of destiny (Smith 1998, 73-76). A sense of destiny is important as it indicates a futuristic possibility of greater fulfilment. To me, India satisfies all the above criteria from prehistory. Rightly or wrongly, we have distinguished ourselves from the "other". The "other" is purely a geographical term and foreigners, either a collective body as tribes or an individual, who have made India their home have been accepted as Indians since our concept of the nation is a territorial and cultural concept, unlike in Europe where nationalism grew from the 17th century onwards with ethnicity, religion and language the focus.

Shyam Saran in his book (*How India Sees the World: Kautilya to the 21st Century*) explains Jambudvipa, or the "four petal lotus" with Bharat Varsha being the southern petal encompassing the Himalayas, river systems and seas on the sides (Saran 2017, 9). Therefore, continental geography is tied to physical geography. And another aspect we can look into is the reason why the Goddess/ Devi at Kanyakumari is unmarried? The belief is that because the Devi at

Kanyakumari could not marry Shiva, contrary to universal Hindu traditions since she might get caught up in domesticity and ignore her primary task of guarding mainland India's southern point. This is a concept or belief that emerged thousands of years ago and therefore to say India was never a nation is wrong.

To give another example, when Alexander came to India he brought historians along with him, the most famous being Strabo, who wrote a book on Indica. In the book he describes India as a rhomboid, an unequal quadrilateral, in shape, with the Indus to the West, the mountains to the North and seas on the East and South. The book further quotes two shramans or sadhus who described the length of the East and West Coast, including their distances. In the 19th century when the British measured the same coast they were surprised to find that the sadhus were off by a few miles only. In other words, we can conclude that 2,200 years ago Indians knew the form and extent of our native land. After all, the Ashokan rock edicts and pillars end at Western Balochistan.

In 1897, with the British consolidating effective control over all of India's traditional geography, the annual session of the Indian National Congress asked the Raj not to deploy Indian troops outside the country's natural borders, indicating a continuity. And Alexander Cunningham who played such an important part in establishing the Archaeological Survey of India, referring to Alexander's conversation with the shramans over 2200 years before pointed to "the close agreement of these dimensions with the actual size of the country is very remarkable and shows that Indians, even at that early date in their history, had a very accurate knowledge of the form and extent of their native land" (Cunningham 1871, 3). After all, all foreigners gave India a common name—the Portuguese called their possessions in India as Estado da India, the French, L'etat de l'Inde. So, the concept of India was present; a geographical and cultural concept and not a political unified entity, but as one which had well-defined components (districts and provinces) known as Janapadas and Mahajanapadas. The larger kingdom or empire may come and go but the local politico-administrative entity carried on. For example, the boundaries of the province of Bihar remained unchanged for millennia till 2003 when, with the creation of the state of Jharkhand, the Rajmahal hills territory went to it.

Indian history has been recorded in terms of political movements as elsewhere and therefore it is important to examine how Indians thought of themselves. One could start with Kautilya. He came from Peshawar in the north west of India and was active in Magadh. He gave us *Arthshastra*—the science of governance, including the relationship with other powers, kingdoms and rulers—the concept of mandala which speaks of a hub and spoke, with the expanding state as the foci of political power. *Arthshastra* is itself drawn from older sources and says that the "welfare of the state depends on an active foreign policy" (Pande 2017, 24). Further, the importance of trade and interdependence is mentioned along with how the state is structured. This is known as the *Saptanga*, or seven-limb theory. These limbs were the political leadership (*svamin*), governance through counsellors (*amatyas*), territory and people (*janapada* or *rashtra*), economy (*kosha*), fortifications (*durga*), military power (*danda*) and allies (*mitras*). As Liebig explains, this theory lays down the raison d'état very comprehensively, covering state-craft, economy, foreign relations, etc. (Liebig et al 2017, 6-7)

This was a multi-polar world where the Mauryas were trying to expand and consolidate power. They faced troubles from others and for them aggression was a form of defence. This approach (Sadgunya theory) is rooted in caution since first they seek peace through a treaty (*sandhi*); then try to stay neutral (*asana*); then march on an expedition (*yana*); seek protection from stronger states (*samshraya*); and finally have a dual policy of war with one state and peace with another (*dvaidhibhava*) (Liebig et. al., 2017, 7). The point is that there is no rigid framework but rather various options available to a ruler to apply for a Kingdom to survive, keeping the four basic instruments of *sama* (conciliation), *dana* (placating, gifts), *danda* (punish using force) and *bheda* (sowing dissensions) constant, at the same time showing that mandala is not static but rather one should not apply various theories mechanically. Therefore, the context is important.

Many years later in *Nitisara*, a book written by Kamandaki, the author refers to older works and their different theories building on Kautilya among others (Saran 2017, 14). He referred to neighbours as potential allies but was cautious to point out that these were not immutable. For him, war was to be a last resort after all options had been exhausted. He wrote in different times from Kautilya, by when the rulers were more established and defending status quo by fending off challenges. The role of the counsel like *Thiruvalluvar* is very important as they provided the distinction between what is attainable and what is not.

Shyam Saran too points to the role of diplomats and diplomacy. According to him, there are three types of diplomats. Firstly, plenipotentiary or those empowered to take decisions, secondly, those with limited or specific powers like ranking diplomats with representational responsibilities and thirdly, the envoy as emissary (Saran 2017, 15). So, what qualities must a diplomat possess? He should be an expert debater, have good memory, be patient, empathetic, speak eloquently, be well versed in military matters, in Shastra, and should be an experienced person who remains calm and maintains secrecy.

In fact, right from the *Hitopadesa*, *Manu Smriti*, *Agni Purana*, *Vishnu Smriti*, *Mahabharata*, *Valmiki Ramayana*, and *Bhagavatam Purana* to the *Narada Purana*, all have large sections about statecraft and external relations. Therefore, it is completely wrong to say that Indians were not thinking about these issues. Most of these texts have one thing in common—that ultimately men are driven by baser instincts. Therefore, rulers should strive to gain what they have not gained, carefully preserve what they have gained, be ready to strike, conceal secrets and ceaselessly explore the weaknesses of foes (Sagar 2015, 67). This may seem cynical but the important point to remember is that the use of violence and misinformation could be condoned only if it was used to preserve a well governed state.

Aparna Pande in her book, *From Chanakya to Modi: The Evolution of India's Foreign Policy*, highlights the fact that Indians always believed that the subcontinent, the triangular lotus petal, to be one entity and formed the Indian "civilisational sphere of influence" (Pande 2017, 6). While Indians had trading relations from Rome, Egypt, Mesopotamia to the Spice Islands of Java and beyond, Indian kings and armies did not seek conquest of lands outside the subcontinent. So, while kings and emperors could defeat and conquer lands within India, trying to do so outside was considered unethical (Pande 2017, 6) with the Chola example being a solitary exception. Therefore, for the ancients, realism and idealism were not two contradictory forces but acted as a continuum. It must be kept in mind that these philosophers and thought-leaders were always conscious of the fact that power could be misused. Therefore, while it is clear that India had a history, we have to briefly examine if Indians had a sense of history. And for that, one should look at specific historical incidents and see how it resonated across time and space.

The Nandas were replaced as the rulers of Magadh by the Mauryas just after Alexander's brief incursion into India. Vishakhadatta wrote a play,

*Mudrarakshasa*, about this transition of rulers approximately seven hundred to thousand years after the event, an outstanding work which has been hailed as a classic. In the 15th century CE, Dhundiraja in the book *Jataka Bharanam* writes a critical review of Mudrarakshasa. The same play was later translated in Tamil in the early 19th century. The British then "discover" Chandragupta (Sandrakottos) in the 20th century and introduce him to contemporary India, since Indians "don't know their own history." The fact is that many of the ancient texts are living documents available to those who seek them, No doubt there are millions more are waiting to be translated since scholarship in Sanskrit and in the classics has become almost a dying tradition. The disruption in the Indian system of knowledge is a recent phenomenon and was due to the rejection of the vernacular for the cosmopolitan, a process initiated by colonialism and accelerated post-independence, wherein the desire to achieve rapid growth, home-grown systems and traditions were seen as irrelevant at best and likely to prevent the march of progress at worst.

So, were Indians closed to the world and was there absence of strategic thinking? Tanham says that while there was trade with the world, there were no Indian ships (Tanham 1992, 137). However, we have enough evidence of a community of Indians in Alexandria in the pre-Christian era; Ashoka's missionaries had known multiple routes to reach different parts of the known world; the Portuguese on reaching Malacca in the 16th Century remarked that they saw tens of thousands of Indians; when a British spy reached Herat in the early 19th century he said the largest single community of traders were Indians. Historians have mentioned that in Kazan, a town in Russia, in the 17th century, goods were priced in two currencies—the rupee and the rouble; Vasco da Gama picked up Majid, an Indian pilot, in Zanzibar who helped him use the monsoon winds to reach India; the best dhows were made in Beypore and the best ships in Gujarat. In fact, Indian ships were sailing across the world from the East Coast of Africa to the South China Sea. Even at present, international shipping is dominated by sailors from India and the Philippines.

In modern India, there were regular appeals to the British to rule as per their principles. Keshub Sen pointed out that the British were not following Christ's doctrine of forgiveness and expressed himself strongly in favour of moral education so that "race antagonism shall perish...all manner of unbrotherly feeling shall forever pass away, and harmony shall prevail among us all" (Collet 1870, 46). He further added that the British must learn from

Asia, be on the side of civilisation and not of barbarism, so that there could be formed a "blessed and world-wide community of God's children. For that indeed is the destiny of our race" (Sagar 2015, 67). What is particularly striking in the statement is the complete absence of rancour, the desire for equality and the conviction that the future would be better.

Swami Vivekananda spoke of the universal brotherhood to Europe and suggested that one must not chase mirages, and seek to possess by hook or crook and that it was only natural that nations rise and fall. Instead he recommended mildness, gentleness, forbearance and tolerance (Sagar 2015, 66). According to him, the raison d'être of India's existence was spiritualism of the human race, for India never believed in cutting the throats of her neighbours (Sagar 2015, 66). Indian liberal thinking of the period, while proclaiming loyalty to the Raj, and using constitutional means to push towards greater Indianisation of the services, expressed themselves in favour of the British showing greater decency in their overseas dealing and living up to their stated principles. Writing about the drain of wealth to Britain from India, Dadabhai Nauroji called his book *Poverty and Un-British Rule in India*, reflecting the same strain that economic exploitation by the Raj was a distortion that should be corrected. Similarly, these Indians condemned the British Opium Trade in China as a "sin on Britain's head and a curse on India."

However, when militant nationalism arose in India, sections of society accepted the need to engage in righteous violence when required. Bankim Chandra Chattopadhyay in Dharamstattva said that there was an underlying need to protect one's country, a feeling which stemmed from patriotism (Sagar 2015, 68). According to him, Europe derived its strength from patriotism, but India should not use patriotism for those purposes, and that the highest form of patriotism was the love for the entire world. How then, does one reconcile devotion to the nation and love of humanity? The two are in contradiction and Bankim's solution was to strive for the highest good for the greatest numbers (Chattopadhyay 2002, 9).

Aurobindo too talked about developing military and political, commercial greatness, intellectual and aesthetic greatness. He was clear that one cannot shrink from aggressiveness but added that violence "was unrighteous when used wantonly" (Ghosh 1997, 1120–21). According to him, India's ultimate mission was to point humanity towards divine equality, which was the source of human liberty, equality and brotherhood. Mahatma Gandhi argued for positive, not passive, non-violence. This would come from absence of fear, not from a sense of helplessness and he advised Europeans to surrender to Hitler. Therefore, he was clear that when the only choice was between cowardice and violence, one should pick violence (Sagar 2015, 70). Tagore warned against exuberant materialism which according to him, led to destruction. He talked about the concept of balance of power as a response to this fear and saw mutual protection arising from this conspiracy of fear. For him, Asia held the answers to global peace, but with Japan and China slipping away from their civilisational moorings, India alone offered hope. India never sailed forth for domination, nor scrambled for spoils. Instead, it offered "a basis for unity which is not power" (Tagore 1917, 107) and yet Tagore was not anti-West. He said that, "when we truly know Europe which is great and good, we will effectively save ourselves from the Europe that is mean and grasping" (Tagore 1917, 107). The message was that India must embrace cosmopolitanism, without forgetting its heritage.

Savarkar, the epitome of Hindu nationalism, is seen as the ultimate realist. Post-World War I, he thought of a World Federation as the ideal outcome. Accepting that political life was scarred by the incessant struggle for existence and survival of the fittest, he advocated balance of power (Sagar 2015, 72). Therefore, he said that we should "befriend those who are likely to serve our country's interests despite the "isms", so long as they serve our interests." He wanted India to cultivate martial ethic, thereby dispelling the notion of being a "mild face." He was against Gandhi's ideas of absolute non-violence and went on to add that "relative non-violence is our creed, we worship the defensive sword as the first saviour of man." Savarkar never promoted an expansionary brand of nationalism, and argued for the cultivation of the martial spirit as an act of deterrence. Again, the point is clear—India would resort to violence if it were so forced.

India's long experience of being colonised meant that a strong feeling of anti-imperialism arose, which arguably persists till the present times. The basic lesson that Indian leaders and thinkers drew from their experience was that exploitation and dominance were the causes of war and therefore the causes must be eliminated. Peace and imperialism could not exist at the same time. The way forward was for a free India to work with other free nations for the establishment of a world order based on freedom and democracy. At the same time, they were not woolly-headed dreamers and realised the need to associate with like countries for mutual defence and economic cooperation.

Article 51 of the Constitution of India states that the Indian government should endeavour to promote international peace and security, maintain just and honourable relations between nations and to foster respect for international law and treaty obligations in dealings of organised peoples and encourage settlements of international disputes by arbitration. The Constituent Assembly debated India's role in the world quite extensively. There was acceptance that India's mission was peace, with non-violence as its creed but not because India was weak. There was considerable debate in promoting peace and disarmament. Conscious of its history, size and cultural attributes, there was a belief in India's manifest destiny (Sagar and Panda 2015, 208). Similarly, there were debates on India's approach to the Cold War, whether it should join the Commonwealth and if India should choose the side of the West, as a last resort, in keeping with the common democratic values, but there was no consensus (Sagar and Panda 2015, 214). In fact, Patel in his letters to Nehru advocated for closer ties with the US and Israel. However, post-Patel, India adopted essentially the Nehru line. With the coming into force of this consensus, debates on these issues effectively stopped for the next forty years when the end of the Cold War changed global material circumstances very substantially. However, the lack of the binary allowed India to carry out course-corrections when required and even plough the lonely furrow when pushed. In an odd reversal of the norm, the praxis was real but anchored in idealism. This can be seen in the initial decision to hold back Rs 55 crore in dues to Pakistan since it was prosecuting a war against India which it reversed when Gandhi sat in fast against it. On the other side were decisions like the accession of Hyderabad and the liberation of Goa.

What then can one say about India's strategic thinking?

The India of the present is very clear of what it wants to be. It wants rapid domestic growth, abolition of poverty, national unity and equality. It is prepared to work with all but will keep its eyes and options open; it has no desire to be in a very close embrace with anybody, is not looking to burning bridges but it is clear that it will not get bullied either. Therefore, it is prepared to stand up and has so demonstrated. India does not see itself as a revisionist power and therefore feels more comfortable in upholding the world order, iniquitous as it may be. Instead, it wants to reform the world order from within, through dialogue and setting up institutions based on equality and openness. It subscribes to the principle that size cannot override everything else. India sees Jambudvipa as one entity, and within its sphere of influence. It knows it is not the centre of the world but it recognises its increasing positioning and is happy to work in bilateral, plurilateral and multilateral settings to promote its national interests. Two, Indian philosophies and schools of thought highlight the importance of context, and it sees "isms" are ultimately just names that need to be looked at through a context. Gandhi was clear that if the choice was between violence and cowardice, his choice was violence. Similarly, Nehru, for example, was a great proponent of non-violence but used action to unify India when faced with no or little choice.

Lastly, the most important component of Indian strategic thinking is the concept of "*ekam sat vipra bahudha vadanti.*" In simple translation, the truth is one but the wise know it by different names. To elaborate, it builds on the importance of context and of non-discrimination by making clear that there are different paths, each valid in its own way. It means that each society or community is entitled to follow its own individual beliefs and traditions, and that no one should be forced to abandon one's own and follow another's. Since all systems are equally valid, there is no question of anyone being superior or inferior to the other. Combined with the belief that the world is one family (*vasudeva kutumbakam*), the Indian world-view is based on equality and non-discrimination. India aspires to be a leading power, to sit on the high table, a reflection of its belief in its civilisational achievements but yet not be a hegemon for that would militate against its core values. In other words, a combination of realism and idealism, not as a balance but as a continuum.

## NOTE

[1]For John Strachey's comment see Saran, S. (2017). *How India Sees the World: Kautilya to the 21st Century.* New Delhi: Juggernaut, p. 10.

## REFERENCES

Aurobindo. (2002). *Bande Mataram.* Pondicherry: Sri Aurobindo Ashram Press.

Chattopadhyay, B. (2002). *Samya,* translated by Bibek Debroy. New Delhi: Liberty Institute.

Cunningham, A. (1871). *The Ancient Geography of India.* London: Trubner & Co.

Karnad, B. (2015). *Why India is not a Great Power (Yet).* Oxford University Press.

Liebig, M. and Mishra, S. Ed (2017). *The Arthaastra in a Transcultural Perspective: Comparing Kautilya with Sun-Zi, Nizam al-Mulk, Barani and Machiavelli.* New Delhi: Pentagon Press with Institute for Defence Study and Analysis (IDSA)

Pande, A. (2017). *From Chanakya to Modi: The Evolution of India's Foreign Policy.* India: HarperCollins India.

Sagar, R. (2015). "Before Midnight: Views on International Relations, 1857–1947." In: D. Malone, C. Mohan and S. Raghavan, ed., *The Oxford Handbook of Indian Foreign Policy.* Oxford: Oxford University Press.

Sagar, R. and Panda, A. (2015). Pledges and Pious Wishes: The Constituent Assembly Debates and the Myth of a "Nehruvian Consensus". *India Review*, 14(2), pp. 203–20.

Saran, S. (2017). *How India Sees the World: Kautilya to the 21st Century.* New Delhi: Juggernaut.

Sen, K. (1904). *Lectures in India.* London, Paris, New York & Melbourne: Cassell and Company, Limited.

Smith, A. (1998). *Nationalism and Modernism: A Critical Survey of Recent Theories of Nations and Nationalism.* London: Routledge.

Tagore, R. *(1917). Nationalism.* India: Macmillan.

Tanham, G. (1992). Indian Strategic Culture. *The Washington Quarterly*, 15(1), pp.129–42.

Tharoor, S. (1997). *India: From Midnight to the Millennium.* New Delhi: Penguin Books.

Vivekananda (1955a). *The Complete Works of Swami Vivekananda*, Vol. 3. Calcutta: Advaita Ashrama.

Vivekananda (1955b). The Complete Works of Swami Vivekananda, Vol. 4. Calcutta: Advaita Ashrama.

# 3

# Panchamrit: The Five Pillars of Indian Foreign Policy

*Ram Madhav*

Foreign Policy, at one level is a continuum as it is transferred from one government to another. However, when Prime Minister Modi took over in 2014, he transformed India's foreign policy in multiple ways. Although the issues and approaches remain the same, the transformation was clearly visible. Today, our foreign policy is bold, proactive, innovative and ambitious.

India's foreign policy is bold as it has shown an uncompromising firmness on issues relating to the nation's integrity and honour. The approach to handling our two neighbours is distinct from what it used to be. The firmness demonstrated in our handling of our relations with Pakistan is a clear indicator. Similarly, with China, whether it was the first ever visit of President Xi Jinping to New Delhi or the recent standoff at Doklam, the government has shown required firmness in conveying a strong message to our eastern neighbour. There are many such examples where firmness has been shown, when India's interests are seen to have been affected by some of their actions. The Prime Minister's decision not to include Maldives in his itinerary during his visit to various island nations in the Indian Ocean Region is a case in point, which highlights the government's bold and firm foreign policy approach.

Traditionally, India has been looked at as a notoriously reticent nation in international affairs. Now, however, it is being seen as proactive in its engagement with the international fora. For example, when countries like the United States of America had changing positions over the Paris Climate Summit, the Indian stand remained steadfast. In fact, India played a crucial role in clinching the

Paris climate deal. Similarly, India has gone ahead and created new forums like the International Solar Alliance and has been proactive in its increased engagement with ASEAN countries. India's active presence in successive G-20 forums has been recognised, as has its greater engagement in Davos. All this shows the present nature of India's foreign policy, which is now no longer reticent and withdrawn but distinctly proactive.

The next transformative feature of India's foreign policy is ambition. In my view, it is for the first time that India has openly shown its ambition to rise as a global power when, during the Prime Minister's first visit to USA, Mr Narendra Modi, along with the then US President Barack Obama, issued a joint statement in which it was mentioned that India has an ambition to rise as an influential and responsible global power. India's rise, along with being influential, will be responsible and peaceful, and will not give anyone sleepless nights. Therefore, an ambitious but responsible rise as a global power is one of India's foreign policy goals.

Foreign policy cannot be romantic or driven by slogans. It must be pragmatic and it has to be blended with a nation's national interests. India has done this with great success and effect. One important aspect of blending foreign policy with national interest is India's policy of de-hyphenation. An emphasis on stand alone and bilateral relations without being influenced by any hyphenated factor is a very unique element that has been introduced into India's foreign policy. It began in 2014 when Prime Minister Modi visited New York to deliver his speech at the United Nations General Assembly. There was a suggestion that he should meet with Prime Minister Netanyahu of Israel. However, as per earlier practises, a standalone meeting with Israeli leadership was not held, unless it was followed with a meeting of the leaders of Palestine. It was Prime Minister Modi who took the decision to end this convention.

Similarly, when leaders would visit India they would balance it with a stopover in Islamabad, regardless of the fact that such a visit to Pakistan was warranted or not. When President Clinton visited India for three whole days, he made a brief stopover in Islamabad for five hours! Visiting both nations together had become a ritual, but now this too has been ended. Standalone visits and bilateral relationships help both countries. When Prime Minister Modi visited Israel recently, he was the first Indian Prime Minister to step on their soil, and the visit was a standalone one. In fact, the Prime Minister will also be embarking on a standalone visit to Palestine in February 2018. For long, India has been a victim of hyphenation. The present government has ended this policy, keeping clear national interests in mind.

India's foreign policy is now also more innovative. Generally, the foreign policy was understood to rest on two important pillars—economic interest and national security. When the BJP came to power, three more pillars were added. As such, India's foreign policy today is guided by the five pillars of 'Panchamrit.' While the first two pillars remain Economic Prosperity and National Security, the third pillar added is 'Samman' or dignity and honour of India. India includes both the citizens of our nation as well as expatriate Indians. Our obligation is to ensure the security, honour and dignity of all Indian citizens, wherever they may be, as well as ensure the dignity, security and honour of India. Four years since 2014, we can confidently say that thanks to the efforts of the entire foreign policy establishment, especially the Foreign Minister and the various missions, we have been able to infuse in individuals, pride in their Indian identity. Today, every Indian feels secure and proud of his Indian identity and his Indian connection. Therefore, 'Samman' is an important dimension.

The next pillar, 'Samvad,' is about greater engagement. Prime Minister Modi and other leaders and officials no longer only meet just their counterparts alone, but a variety of stakeholders. Engagement on multiple levels from government to government, government to business, government to people, government to academics, scholars and the diaspora exist. This wider engagement has been made a dimension of India's foreign policy approach.

A special attention has been given to engagement with the diaspora. This has helped us in creating fronts across the spectrum in academia and other spheres. As far as the diaspora itself is concerned, it has definitely helped us in two ways. First, the diaspora was and continues to be a divided diaspora, but the government's efforts has helped in creating larger unity within the diaspora community. As a member of the BJP, there used to be a temptation to hold Overseas Friends of BJP events when the Prime Minister went abroad. We were however instructed, that the Prime Minister's event will be for the entire diaspora and will not be restricted to those who support the party. This has helped in creating greater unity within the diaspora community. Through that unity, the diaspora has been able to rise as a political constituency in their respective countries. This will help India in different ways. These efforts have also helped in establishing a good and live contact between the diaspora and the main Indian territory. This neatly ties in with the fifth pillar—Sanskriti—using our cultural and civilisational links as a tool of our foreign policy.

In the past, foreign policy had shied away from using our cultural and civilisational wealth as its tool, as it was assumed that culture cannot be included in order to have a secular foreign policy. Under the Modi government, these have been converted into effective instruments of our foreign policy. The Japanese Prime Minister went to Varanasi and did a Ganga Aarti and the Chinese Premier participated in local festivals in Gujarat. Similarly, Prime Minister Modi visited the Pashupatinath temple in Nepal, a mosque in central Asia, a church or synagogue elsewhere and even played traditional drums in one country! This aspect of making cultural and civilisation wealth of our country an effective diplomatic tool is an important hallmark of our foreign policy. Along with Samriddhi (economic prosperity) and Suraksha (security), we have created a robust five-pronged approach to India's foreign policy.

Finally, in our neighbourhood we gave the call, 'together we grow.' We built confidence in our neighbours that India's rise will help in the rise of our neighbours and vice versa. The Prime Minister gave this call in Bhutan, Nepal and Bangladesh. He spoke to the nations as sovereign equals and not as a big brother.

India's foreign policy has for a long time been land based as we have traditionally been Westward looking, and therefore our interests have been linked to European and American interests. We have now introduced the policy of ocean-centric approach. Looking to the East calls for a change in our thinking as our issues are different. This change has come about over the last three to four years. Today, we value our relationship with ASEAN countries as much as we value our relationship with the European Union or USA. Hence, we had all the 10 heads of ASEAN as guests of honour in the 2017 Republic Day Parade. This was done even though some of the countries are small and do not have much dealings with India, such as Laos and Cambodia. The change is underway. India has moved from its policy of 'Look East' to 'Act East,' because we believe that the 21st century global power has shifted from the Pacific region to the Indian Ocean region.

In conclusion, India's emphasis on its 'Act East' policy has finally led to the Western world accepting the centrality and primacy of the Indian Ocean to 21st century geopolitics, and for the first time, the West has started using the phrase Indo-Pacific instead of Asia-Pacific. A case in point is President Trump articulating the phrase Indo-Pacific, as we have made it our foreign policy objective and priority. Today, India's foreign policy is bold, proactive, ambitious and innovative.

# 4

## Impact of War

*Alok Bansal*

What is War? Clausewitz defined war as "...the continuation of politics by other means". Avoidance of war is also a very powerful diplomatic tool. If you go by what Sun Tzu said, "The supreme art of war is to subdue the enemy without fighting". With these two basic definitions or quotations in place, how does war impact diplomacy and foreign policy. War brings a sense of urgency to any diplomatic manoeuvre, because when there is a war, there is a sense of self-preservation, and also at times, we find opportunities. Historically, there are certain instances that dictate a sense of urgency during times of war. Nations make alliances and diplomatic moves. They decide on certain moves based on their perceived national interest, which off course countries do all the time; but in times of war such moves assume added urgency with the hope that results would be instantaneous or at least expected in the short term. Consequently, we find that nations make very, very strange choices. For example, before World War I, there was the Triple Alliance which comprised Kaiser's Germany, the Austro-Hungarian Empire and Italy. But when the War began, the Kingdom of Italy, which was part of the Triple Alliance, actually joined the other side and became a part of the Allied cause. This occurred because Italy quickly realised that it had more to gain by joining the Allied powers as certain territories of Italy were occupied by the Austro-Hungarian Empire. Despite a treaty obligation and being part of an alliance, Italy chose a different course and claimed that it had joined the Triple Alliance only as a defensive manoeuvre. As the Austro-Hungarian Empire had declared war against Serbia after the assassination of its Archduke Ferdinand, Italy felt it had the right to renege on the earlier alliance. That is how war can have an impact on a country's foreign policy.

Let us now look at the Indian context and see how wars have shaped India's Foreign Policy. As soon as India got its independence, it was embroiled in the Kashmir conflict. This particular conflict shaped India's foreign policy for a very long time with India assuming the moral and legal high ground. India had Constitutional sanctity with respect to Kashmir and as a result, the then prime minister, Jawahar Lal Nehru took the issue to the United Nations (UN). The UN Resolution of 1948 asked Pakistan to vacate Jammu & Kashmir and hand it back to India. Thereafter, the resolution called upon India to hold a plebiscite to determine the wishes of the people. Pakistan did not vacate its occupied areas and so no plebiscite could be held. In any case, as time passed, the global geopolitics too changed and we found Cold War dynamics coming into play. Consequently, much to its chagrin, India found the Western powers voting against India at the UN and exerting pressure to yield on J&K. This was the period when support to India on the Kashmir issue came from the Warsaw pact countries and the Soviet Union. Consequently, India's criticism of the Soviet Union was muted, when Soviet forces invaded Budapest and other regions, to quell the Hungarian uprising of 1956.

Another important landmark in Indian foreign policy was the liberation of Goa in 1961. In terms of foreign policy, this was a significant event as Portugal's Salazar government had declared Goa to be a province of Portugal, and not a colony. Portugal was a member of NATO, whose charter mandated that any attack on its members would be repelled by NATO. Earlier, in 1955, India had imposed economic sanctions on Goa, but these sanctions had little impact as Goa was surrounded by the seas and thus could be maintained by Portugal, which also had the support of other nations. India however, did manage to free Dadra and Nagar Haveli through such sanctions. President Eisenhower's government was firmly with Portugal, but in early 1961, the Democrats won the elections, with John F. Kennedy narrowly defeating the Republican nominee, Richard Nixon. In December 1961, in a swift operation, Goa was liberated by the Indian Army, in an operation that lasted barely 40 hours. It is important to note that in the UNSC, virtually every country opposed the Indian action, and called for a resolution asking Indian forces to vacate Goa. The Soviet veto, however, prevented the passage of this resolution. In the then 11-member UNSC, only the USSR and Sri Lanka supported India. US-India relations soured with the then representative of the US making very disparaging remarks about India. Fortunately for India, a series of other important events took centre stage, and as US-Soviet relations were tense,

NATO did not come into play. But, it was this conflict that impinged on India's foreign policy in 1962. To India's advantage was the fact that when Indian forces moved into Goa in December 1961, the attention of the Western world was still focussed on the failed Bay of Pigs invasion the US had attempted to overthrow Fidel Castro of Cuba. Also, as the war was over in less than two days, NATO's "collective defense" clause could not be brought into operation as the Portuguese forces had surrendered.

The 1962 Sino-India War not just changed, but dictated India's foreign policy. In fact, Mr Nehru wrote letters to the US, the UK and Soviet Russia requesting for military assistance. There was a drastic foreign policy shift post the war. During the war, the Western powers put immense pressure on Pakistan and forced it to desist from attacking India in Kashmir. Subsequently, after the war, there was pressure on India to yield Kashmir to Pakistan. The weakest position of India with respect to J&K was between 1962 and 1965. Certain resolutions, official and media reports say that India was in fact ready to concede some territory across the Line of Control (LoC). This war also caused tensions in Sino-Soviet relations. More importantly, the aftermath of the war resulted in China and Pakistan getting close to each other. The Sino-Pakistan Agreement of 1963 was a direct implication of the Sino-Indian conflict of 1962, and was premised on the dictum 'your enemy's enemy is your friend'. This is what made Pakistan, which at that point of time was a member of the Western military alliances, dabble with Communist China, which was not even recognised by the West.

Post the 1965 India-Pakistan war, and the Tashkent Agreement, India vacated large tracts of land it had captured from Pakistan. This action was severely criticised by military historians, but perhaps was dictated by the geo-political situation existing at that time. The Western World was against India on the Kashmir issue and was exerting pressure on India to yield to Pakistani demands. India's support came from the USSR, which was arbitrating between the two countries and that left India little room for manoeuvre. In addition, India was ravaged by a severe famine in 1965 and was dependant on American wheat supplies through PL 480, which was keeping the Indian population afloat. While India had the edge when a ceasefire was declared, the 1965 war was not a spectacular military victory for India, but was more in the nature of a stalemate, though India certainly had an edge. However, when the international community demanded that India return to the status quo, India had little option but to oblige.

The 1971 Liberation War was a significant event. The international community paid little heed to the millions of refugees pouring into India from East Pakistan, to escape the brutalities of the Pakistan army. It took some creative diplomacy to even bring Bangladesh to centre-stage, at least in the global consciousness. It took a concert by John Harrison conducted with Pt. Ravishankar to draw attention to the plight of the Bengali population in East Pakistan, as also the visit of Senator Kennedy to the refugee camps established by India for the hapless refugees for the world to take note of the genocide being conducted by Pakistan. The US government as also the Western world, however, refused to support India and was firmly with Pakistan, but support was forthcoming from the public. The Indian armed forces intervened militarily on 3 December 1971 in support of Bangladesh and in a swift 13-day war, forced the Pakistani army in East Pakistan to surrender, leading to the birth of Bangladesh. All through the War, the UNSC voted against India, and it took three Soviet vetoes to keep the UN from passing any resolution. Even Yugoslavia, which was considered a soulmate and was a cofounder of the Non Aligned Movement, voted against India. Other than the Warsaw Pact nations and Bhutan, everyone voted against India, which indicated the extent to which India had been isolated. That was why India declared a unilateral ceasefire on the Western front, once Bangladesh was freed. Media reports and correspondence from that period indicate that there was immense pressure from the USSR to quickly end the war. Bangladesh was soon recognised by the Warsaw Pact countries and Bhutan. It took a bit longer for the western world to acknowledge the new reality.

The last major conflict that India engaged in was the Kargil conflict. Unlike previous conflicts, this time the international community was firmly with India and even China was not very supportive of Pakistan. Military pressure by India forced Pakistan to set up a meeting with President Clinton and they eventually had to withdraw from the areas they had intruded into. Wars are thus are nothing but a continuation of policy by other means. But because of its nature, there is a sense of urgency in policies. Mr Nehru's non-alignment ideals were jettisoned as soon as the Chinese attacked India in 1962, forcing him to write for help to the Western powers. Wars, thus, have a phenomenal impact on a country's foreign policy and that has been the experience of India.

# 5

# Securing the Nation

*Shekhar Sinha*

India's foreign policy has not been a matter of public debate in this country. Even after the nation has fought a war, there has been limited public discourse. A reason why such issues are not discussed in the public domain is perhaps due to the fact that India does not have an articulated public national security strategy, which most democratic countries tend to publish. Even China has a document of that kind. However, the absence of a written document does not mean that India does not have a national security perspective. There are institutions within the government and outside it, which constantly evaluate the security environment and deliberate with those who have to craft out diplomatic and defence policy agendas and framework.

War, as defined by the Oxford English Dictionary, is a state of armed conflict between countries or different groups within a country. It further states that it is a state of hostility between different people or groups, within or outside the country. This definition in the Indian context implies the following:

- Wars fought by India with Pakistan and the India-China conflict of 1962, where the militaries of the respective countries were engaged in combat.
- Internal armed conflict, such as that prevailing in parts of Northeast India, J&K and in some of the districts of India affected by Left Wing Extremism (LWE).
- Wars against the drug mafias.

The above are all wars of a different kind. Apart from the armed military conflicts, there are a number of systemic conflicts in the larger geo-political domain, which have impacted on India's foreign policy. An example is the

Cold War, which led to India's policy of non-alignment. The end of the Cold War following the break up of the Soviet Union also had its ramifications on India's foreign policy. Asymmetric warfare, low-intensity conflict, cyber warfare, information warfare, etc., have to be factored in to the nations security policy and its foreign policy framework, as do the possibility of larger and more destructive instruments such as nuclear, biological and chemical warfare. While the nation's prosperity must always be the primary goal of any foreign policy, such prosperity needs to be protected by appropriate security measures. Various ways have been adopted by the Indian state to achieve these objectives.

Foreign policy is shaped and directed by political leadership or by individuals, based on their understanding of geopolitics and their vision of how a specific worldview can be accommodated, for the benefit of the people whom they represent. Perforce, they would have to look into not just the situation as existing in their own country but in the region and the whole world itself. While the military perspective is important, it cannot be the only consideration and multiple factors would require consideration in the formulation of policy.

In essence, three factors drive national interest, and in turn a nation's foreign policy. The first is the geopolitical context. Second is the economic and developmental needs within the country, and third is the defence of the country and maintaining its territorial integrity, to include not just land territory, but also the air space, the EEZs and other areas where legal rights are exercised.

The Indo-China war of 1962 brought home a clear lesson that there are no permanent friends. This war shattered the myth 'Hindi-Chini Bhai Bhai,'— a popular slogan in the decade before the 1962 war. What this war brought out was that in the pursuit of national interest, a country will not be averse to waging war. The Dalai Lama's exit to India had in a way made China think that India had the potential to brew trouble in Tibet. The war was a message to India that China will use force to protect its perceived national interest. Recent events, such as in Doklam on the Bhutan-Tibet border or Chinese actions in the South China Sea have shown that China will use force or will threaten the use of force to settle its disputes. This has made India seek foreign collaboration with technologically advanced countries for the purchase and manufacture of modern weapon systems to counter military threats. Such engagement during the Cold War years took place with the Soviet Union and now, post the Cold War, such engagements are taking place with Russia and a number of technologically advanced Western powers, to maintain an appropriate deterrence and dissuasion capability.

Since 2014, India has proactively engaged with China, without succumbing to Chinese military pressure. At the same time, India continues to cooperate with China on issues of mutual concern such as climate change and along with China, is a member of various organisations such as the Solar Alliance, AIIB, SCO, BRICS and so on. India's foreign policy with respect to China, hence reflects both a collaborative approach as well as a firm, independent approach. The emphasis is on building infrastructure and achieving higher levels of self sufficiency in defence production capabilities. India's Act East policy, which is an important component of India's foreign policy, is reflective of both an economic agenda as well as a security agenda. By linking infrastructure development on the border with the development of the states in Northeast India, the twin objectives of security and development are given an impetus through the Act East policies, to address both India's economic as well as security concerns. On nuclear issues too, we have a common position with China. Both aim for a nuclear free world, have a 'No First Use' Policy and no use of nuclear weapons against a non-nuclear state. India clearly has adopted a non-intrusive, non-expansionist approach, but with zero tolerance to terrorism. These are the impact of War and subsequent events.

The two basic pillars which underline India's foreign policy are Samriddhi (economic prosperity) and Suraksha (security). These are being pursued in a bold and proactive manner. Today, India's bilateral and multi-lateral engagements have two security underpinnings. These relate to maritime security for trade and the need for eliminating all forms of terrorism. The discourse has shifted to give primacy to these two aspects and the media too reflects this reality. News headlines are centred on security issues, from amongst the many agreements signed. For example, at the Delhi ASEAN Summit, most newspapers' headlines stated, 'Delhi Declaration calls for counter-terrorism and maritime security,' thus choosing to highlight this aspect from amongst the many that were signed. That itself marks a significant change, as security issues are now the centre of most discourses. Such a situation was not existing even five years ago. India's ASEAN engagement and Act East Policy clearly demonstrate economic and security imperatives, which itself is a very bold move.

In terms of India's policy with respect to Pakistan, post the 1965 war with Pakistan and later post the Liberation War of 1971 and the Shimla Agreement,

India firmly announced that it will not allow any third party intervention on the Kashmir issue. India enhanced its relations with the Soviet Union, buying oil, arms, technology and heavy industries—all in rupee terms and not in dollars. This marked an important change in foreign policy, dictated by security concerns. It must be remembered that at this time, both China and the US, as also most Western countries were supportive of Pakistan. Our foreign policy at that time was aimed at persuading these countries to remain neutral as far as Indo-Pakistan relations were concerned. The strength of the Soviet veto was an enabling factor in the 1971 Liberation War, though the US did threaten to send the USS Enterprise to the war zone. Fortunately, the war ended quickly with the surrender of the Pakistan Army in East Pakistan, as the Soviet Union too was under pressure and could not have used its veto in the UN indefinitely.

It was China's placement of nuclear weapons on the Tibetan plateau and the US manoeuvres in the Bay of Bengal during the 1971 War that made India determined to build nuclear weapons. India carried out its first nuclear test in May 1974, calling it a peaceful nuclear explosion. Later, in 1998, under the leadership of Atal Bihari Vajpayee, India once again tested its nuclear weapons. Pakistan responded with nuclear tests of its own, and using nuclear power as a deterrent, started to use terrorism as an instrument of its foreign policy. This in turn reshaped India's foreign policy, with appropriate responses at the Line of Control to Pakistani acts of spreading terror on Indian soil.

Post the Cold War, India was seen as being outside the perceived shadow of Soviet Russia and it led to the restructuring of economic and security policies. 'Look East' policy of 1991, and the present Act East policy are signs of India's concerns of the happenings in the Indian Ocean region, as the Indian Ocean is emerging as the fulcrum of economic activity. In the region, India is being viewed as the 'Net Security Provider' which is an important development as it places India in the centre of geopolitics of the world. India seeks constructive engagement and non-interference in others internal affairs but will not hesitate to give a timely and quick intervention as far as national security is concerned. While domestic issues should not hamper foreign policy matters, internal security concerns will always impact on foreign policy. Today, India's 'Neighbourhood First' policy and 'SAGAR' is a very strong and emerging principle. Stress is also on achieving self-sufficiency in defence production, as repeatedly emphasised by Prime Minister Narendra Modi. Therefore, 'Make in India' is one big step in this direction.

# 6

## Contemporary Security Challenges

*Alok Joshi*

India's contemporary security challenges could be encapsulated in the language of Twitter as a factor of internal political dynamics in India's neighbourhood, coupled with rising Chinese interest in the South Asian Region, and the predictable unpredictability of the Trump administration. With these emerge a set of concomitant factors which impact on India's security concerns and throw up challenges for India's foreign policy.

A major consideration is the geo-political challenge arising out of a phased US withdrawal from Afghanistan which will have huge security implications for India as the Taliban has not yet been neutralised. Also of concern is the increasing power projection in the region by the People's Republic of China (PRC), through its interventions in Sri Lanka, Nepal, Maldives, Bangladesh, Pakistan and Myanmar. The Belt and Road Initiative (BRI) of China is also a matter of concern as a major component of the BRI is the China-Pakistan Economic Corridor (CPEC), which aims to link Kashgarh in China's autonomous Xinjiang region to Gwadar in Pakistan that passes though Indian territory in J&K which is under Pakistani occupation. While China claims that the BRI is simply an economic initiative, it is widely viewed as aiming to break perceived US 'encirclement' in the Indo-Pacific and also to constrain the rise of India. Chinese projects in the neighbourhood thus have more of a strategic thrust rather than any economic content that would truly benefit the recipient country. It is also increasingly becoming clear that the massive infrastructure projects promised by the PRC would either leave the recipient countries indebted or bankrupt their economies. We are already seeing the impact it has had on Sri Lanka. This shift in the geo-political landscape can perhaps best be countered by the concept of collective security.

An important aspect of India's national security is increasing the relevance for India of the maritime domain and the Indian Ocean Region (IOR). When India started economic reforms in 1991, her external merchandise trade accounted for less than 18 percent of GDP. By 2014, in proportion it has risen to almost 50 per cent of GDP and well over 80 per cent of that trade is carried out by sea. This gives an idea of the importance of the Indian Ocean to India's security and economic well-being. Fortunately, the security situation in Indian Ocean is not as acute as in the South China Sea, which has a spate of territorial or maritime disputes or even the distant Pacific, where there is a struggle for neo-dominance. The Indian Ocean's issues arise mainly from troubles on land, particularly around its choke points, and the resulting piracy and instability that threaten the security and safety of critical sea links. Fifty per cent of world's trade passes through crucial choke points in the IOR and its sea links carry a large proportion of the world's energy flows. The open geography of the Indian Ocean means that no single power can or is likely to dominate it. But this does not prevent us from trying and this certainly would affect India's security issues.

Increasing Chinese naval presence in the Indian Ocean is a concern for India's maritime security. In 2013, when piracy along the Somalian coast was a major concern, there was an increased presence of foreign navies as part of anti-piracy operations. This was the time when the Chinese sent a submarine for operations in the Indian Ocean and explained it as part of the anti-piracy operation. If such flimsy excuses can be used to send submarines into the region, then it is a matter of serious concern for India.

Extremist Islamic radicalism is also a matter of concern to India, as India has a large expatriate population working in the gulf countries. There is a danger that some of these people may come back to India imbued with radical ideology. As of now, the recruitment of Indians into the cadres of the ISIS has been minimal, and till 2017, only about 75-80 individuals had joined that organisation. The ISIS also stands depleted with largely reduced territorial control. But the threat of the spread of the ideology propagated by the ISIS and which has an attraction for the youth. That remains a challenge to ensure that the idea does not catch momentum here in India.

Another issue of concern to India is the potential flow of refugees into the country. India has been host to refugees whenever there has been a crisis in the neighbourhood, as seen by the millions of refugees who poured into India in

1971 from Bangladesh, following the Pakistani military crackdown in erstwhile East Pakistan. In the present context, the Rohingya crisis has created concerns within the country, particularly as the background of radicalisation has been there among the Rohingya starting from 2011-12 period. We have about 40-45 thousand Rohingya refugees in India which is a cause for concern.

In addition to the above, India also has concerns with respect to conventional threats. Of major concern is the issue of cyber security, where the threat is asymmetrical. It cannot be measured man to man or technology to technology. This is also a field where the concept of deterrence does not work because the source from where the threat emanates cannot be determined. India's critical information infrastructure is vulnerable because it developed in a very inorganic way, unlike the PRC which had systems in place right from the word go, which ensured homogeneity. The threat to India is palpable and is one area which is going to be increasingly of concern.

The internal dynamics of the countries in India's neighbourhood also impinge on India's security. To India's west is Pakistan, which has consistently used terrorism against India as an instrument of its foreign policy. The terrorist infrastructure within Pakistan is intact and the state supports a huge terrorist infrastructure and provides support to terrorist organisations in terms of training, provision of weapons and equipment, intelligence and administrative support and facilitates their infiltration into India. The JeM and LeT, both terrorists organisations based in Pakistan and focussed against India remain matters of grave concern to India's security. In the first three quarters of 2017, we had 358 persons trying to enter J&K out of which 218 were terrorists, 83 were security personnel and 27 were civilians. This number was the second highest since 2010. Apart from this, Pakistani troops repeatedly violate the ceasefire agreement with as many as 600 ceasefire violations taking place in 2107 up to end September. Ceasefire violations by Pakistan have led to loss of lives in India's security forces, and this hostility by Pakistan will remain a matter of concern, for some time. While a civilian government does exist in Pakistan, it is too weak to rein in the Pakistani military establishment, which thrives on an anti-India stance.

Also of concern is the increasing restiveness on the India-China border. This is another security challenge that we will have to face in the coming days. Doklam was one of the symptoms; but in the days ahead we will have to see how we manage our relationship with China as far as the Sino-Indian border is concerned. I also see a continuum of threat from China and Pakistan, and India cannot afford to look at the threats coming from these two countries in isolation from each other. This is increasingly becoming evident by the number of joint exercises being conducted by these two countries, which is of critical strategic concern to us. Today, about 70 per cent to 80 per cent of the equipment of the Pakistan army is of Chinese origin. The aspect of interoperability between the two militaries will have to be taken into account along with the joint exercises being conducted by the special forces and the navies of the two countries. This is a situation which India will have to manage. Increasingly, India would be looking at a collective security architecture in the region and certain initiatives in this regard have been increased cooperation with ASEAN and the Quad in the IOR.

# 7

## Key Security Concerns

*R.N. Ravi*

Prime Minister Narendra Modi has articulated the essence of India's foreign policy in many forums, the most recent being at Davos in January 2018, where he addressed the 48th World Economic Summit. The way we look at the world, he said, is encompassed in the expression 'Vasudhaiva Kutumbakam,' a sanatan (eternal) worldview propounded in Hindu texts such as the *Upanishad*, which means 'the world is one family.' The Prime Minister went on to state that a well known legacy of India's spiritual and intellectual tradition encapsulating the pan-humanity inter-relation in the Indian Vedic verse, 'Om Saha Naav[au]-Avatu (together we are protected), Saha Nau Bhunaktu (together we prosper), Saha Viiryam Karavaavahai (Together we work towards the glory of mankind), Tejasvi Naav[au]-Adhiitam-Astu Maa Vidvissaavahai (Let no poison of hatred infect any ones mind).' That indeed has been the Indian tradition that permeates in India's culture. With this outlook, India must also gain its rightful place in the comity of nations and play its rightful role as a responsible power on the world stage. For that to come about, India has perforce to be economically and militarily strong and anything that impedes this vision becomes a national security concern. From the foreign policy perspective, I will focus on two such concerns, one an existing concern and the other a threat that is looming.

The main obstacle to India's growth is China's unremitting hostile orientation towards India. China looks at India as an adversary and consequently does everything possible to undermine its potential.

On the other hand, India has consistently supported China and helped it secure its rightful place, be it political liberation, membership of the UN, at the WTO and at each and every forum. The Indian establishment has consistently underplayed and even tried to overcome the setbacks of 1962 by maintaining a tranquility on the Line of Actual Control (LAC), despite intermittent provocative transgressions by the PLA. The Indian response has been primarily aimed at making China comfortable and to indicate to the Chinese leadership that India holds no extra-territorial ambitions. To that extent, India even neglected the development of infrastructure along the border with Tibet, though that came at a cost to India's border population. China, on the other hand, built its infrastructure right up to the LAC, at an exponential rate.

India's hope was that being great civilisational powers, both India and China had a common goal of pulling their respective people out of poverty. Both the countries shared a common experience of humiliation by foreign powers, and it was hoped that both could work like partners in progress. But hope, as India sadly found, is not a panacea for foreign policy. China has been consistent with its policy of waging proxy war on India and has sought to destabilise both the Northeastern frontier of India by equipping and encouraging ethnic rebels in India's northeast and has also encouraged Pakistan to maintain a hostile attitude towards India through support to Pakistan in the military and strategic sphere. In the Northeast, China has since 1965 provided material and logistic support to Naga rebels and also to other insurgent groups, and continues to encourage and shelter them to continue raising proxy war on India. It is the Chinese technology which helped Pakistan maintain nuclear parity with India, and it is Chinese efforts which deny India access to the Nuclear Suppliers Group (NSG). Through its Belt and Road Initiative (BRI), China has run roughshod over India's concerns and is actively engaged with Pakistan in building the China-Pakistan Economic Corridor (CPEC), which passes through that part of the state of J&K which is under Pakistan's illegal occupation.

India has been addressing the issue of insurgency in the Northeast through political, administrative and military measures, as a result of which the security situation has shown a remarkable improvement. Till a few years back, there were over 1000 fatalities in insurgency related violence in the North-East every year. This figure has dipped dramatically, and in 2017 stood at below 50 fatalities. Though there is an overall improvement, China has once again become very active in consolidating various insurgent groups, forging a common operational platform to give them a greater capacity to strike. It is out to sabotage the Naga negotiation by creating public order situations, by encouraging the groups to come together and even by instigating the Naga rebels to walk out of the negotiations.

Another matter of concern is China's attempts to undermine the political integrity of South Asia by pursuing a policy of neo-colonialism, through development of unproductive mega projects and infrastructure and leading such countries into debt traps. China exploits the inadequate expertise, legal, technical and financial in these countries to evaluate objectively the impact and implication of these projects. Since these countries lack this capacity, China has succeeded in pushing its predatory economic policies.

An example is the construction of the Gwadar Port in Pakistan. When Pakistan's Mir Qasim and Karachi ports are not functioning even to half of their capacity, it makes little commercial sense to make a third port. Once Pakistan is saddled with debt, China will in all likelihood make Gwadar a base for Chinese naval operations. We have seen what happened in Hambantota in Sri Lanka. Gwadar will be no different. China is also attempting to do the same in Kyaukpyu in Myanmar, where it has promised USD 10 billion as investment selling a dream of making Kyaukpyu as Singapore or Hong Kong. It is evident that a strategic geometry is being shaped, with Gwadar, Hambantota and Kyaukpyu, through unethical means. Recently, Bangladesh has blacklisted China Harbour Engineering Company, which runs most of China's overseas activities in this region, as the firm offered Tk 5 million (USD 60,000) in bribes to the communication secretary. In Sri Lanka, China built a power plant for USD 1.3 billion, but the country is having problems in repaying the loan. When the country asked China to take equity in lieu, China re-evaluated the project at 2/3rd of the cost at which it was built, conveniently siphoning off half a billion! And when the power plant develops intermittent problems, it is the Chinese workforce which sits there complacently. China has deeply infiltrated into the mass media communication network of these countries and emasculated the will of these countries to take autonomous decisions. Many of India's neighbours have been impacted, with China acquiring the stakes in the print and electronic media. The Internet Service Providers from China, are now routing the consumer data through China, by placing the servers there. Some of these platforms are aggregators and disseminators. China regulates the traffic and also filters and moderates the same.

In the Indian Ocean, China has greatly expanded its naval presence, with sophisticated naval warships including nuclear submarines operating in these waters. A submarine base is being built in Bangladesh, though Bangladesh has only two submarines. It is also trying to seed the Indian Ocean bed with satellite-linked sensors. With the Maldives, an MoU has been signed for seeding its entire Exclusive Economic Zone with sensors and buoys on the surface and satellite above. The next stage would be in other countries, obviously to make a China-centric world order. This has serious security implications for India.

Another looming concern is our capacity to deal with fifth generation warfare. This term is used for wars, where non-state warriors fight nation states out of sheer frustration without clear political objectives and is an interesting development. This will be a far more complicated challenge for India. In an increasingly networked world, where the domain of internet of things is fast expanding, the possibility of a multi-domain conflict is not unreal. Such a war is to be fought in cooperation with like-minded countries. India, besides building its capacity, will also have to go in for cooperative structures within the region and across the globe, to prepare for such eventualities.

# 8

# Building Credibility

*S. Jaishankar*

All the changes that we are seeing in the world today—the rise of China, events in the US and Middle East and India's growing influence—are part of a process. Hence, it is important to always keep the context in mind. The present international system can be traced back to the breakup of the Soviet Union, the so-called "triumph" of the Western world followed by the rise of Asia and the growth of political Islam. These events created a flatter world, eroding traditional camps and making decision making a much harder process. Therefore, we need to ask ourselves how relevant and adequate non-alignment and strategic autonomy are when India itself seeks to be a fixed point and as the world becomes truly multipolar.

For the neighbourhood, we generally use the term "Neighbourhood First." The term means we give our neighbourhood a priority, a degree of attention, care, consideration, resources and energy. None of this should be confused with optimism. This kind of attention has not been given by previous policy makers. For instance, in Bangladesh alone, our commitments increased from around USD 800 million in 2011 to around USD 8 billion today. The second aspect of Neighbourhood First is regionalism. We have not always approached regionalism confidently in the past but today, we are big, secure and confident enough to develop regionalism non-reciprocally. It is in our interest that our neighbours share and grow with the prosperity of India. The third feature is the impact of China. If China is to become a global power it is only natural that it will exert its influence and it will be strongest in the region closest to China. Therefore, we should not be alarmed by the fact that China's influence in South Asia is increasing. Instead we should focus on whether the influence is good or bad and how to respond to it. We need to work with powers with whom we have converging interests.

Our next policy angle is the shift from Look East to Act East. The two big new elements in our eastern policy are stronger emphasis on physical connectivity and security. If roadways, shipping lanes and rail lines open up towards Vietnam, the entire politics, economics and sociology of that region will change. We have for years allowed the status quo to prevail, even rationalising it to somehow be good for India's security. We often joke that the first step of "Look East" is New Delhi having to look east to other parts of India! Unfortunately, the Centre has not adequately done this. However, this is changing and today we are actively thinking about how to promote India's Northeast region and make it a fulcrum of Act East policy. In fact, Bangladesh can play an important role—its infrastructure can be used to service eastern India's economy—which is why we have put a lot of effort to modernise railways, power connectivity and waterway usage through Bangladesh. The next aspect is security. If you look at the ferment in the Islamic world, that ferment comes upto the Punjab but abruptly stops at the "wall" called India. This wall insulates the entire ferment that is coming from Nigeria all the way up to Pakistan's Punjab. If there are today Islamic societies like Indonesia, Malaysia and Brunei that have relatively been sheltered from the disturbances of the Middle East and beyond, it is in large part because India has absorbed those pressures. For us, security cooperation, both military and intelligence cooperation, is a very important feature of our relationship with Southeast Asian countries. In fact, hosting all the ten ASEAN heads of state is a recognition of the fact that ASEAN itself is graduating into a different level of cooperation with us.

Looking to the West, India has always strongly emphasised on the Gulf. With countries like UAE, Qatar and Saudi Arabia, our relations were good but were not fully reflective of the interests of those countries or India's potential. This is something that has changed. Here, the challenge for India is that the Gulf is very much a region in ferment, but a region with which we have high economic and energy dependency. It must be borne in mind that the remittances India receives from the Gulf is roughly the size of its services trade with America. Therefore, just looking at the quantitative aspect it should become clear of how important the Gulf is and should be. For us, stability in the Gulf is very important and managing a policy with multiple pulls and pressures is of our greatest concern. When we were a smaller power we could afford to stay away from difficult regions but that option is no longer available to us.

Afghanistan and Pakistan remain a key security challenge for India. A great deal of progress has been made in the security situation in Afghanistan, though a large part of the progress made has been underestimated, partly due to very bad handling of these countries by the previous American administrations supplemented by NATO powers. The fact remains that there were serious misreadings of the situation. Yet, the reality is that people in Afghanistan welcome the change and India remains a very popular country in Afghanistan. It is popular because our image in Afghanistan is of a developmental partner; a country that has largely listened to the Afghans and contributed to a more stable life. For us today, stabilising Afghanistan is of paramount importance. The reality today is that there isn't an Afghan problem but an Af-Pak problem. The heart of the problem lies in Pakistan and there is more recognition of this aspect in parts of the Western world.

The rise of China has been one of the biggest developments in our lifetime. We have to recognise that we have as a neighbour, a major influencer with whom we have a very complex history and differences in interests but one that is also our second largest trade partner and fastest growing investor. It is however not smart analysis to be either in denial of or to demonise China. The rise of a global power is accompanied by the creation of new institutions. China is, in a departure from the past, suggesting itself as a model. Its viability is an open question. We traditionally thought of China as a power to our North but we must also begin to look at China's maritime presence in the Indian Ocean.

There has been a sharper sense of maritime spaces in our foreign policy. The fact is the Indian Ocean has historically been a community, the people of the region have an interpenetrative culture, it is the largest English speaking lake in the world and much of it is democratic. There is a need to grow the Indian Ocean into something more substantive than it is today.

As for the United States, its decline has been repeatedly foretold but it continues to surprise the world with its ability to reinvent itself and find new sources of strength. In my opinion, the US is still the only global power and will remain so for a number of years. The US derives its strength from being the greatest centre of innovation and technology. Therefore, the protection of Intellectual Property Rights has become central to American policy. Moreover, the US is now conveying to its allies that its terms are different and has become more demanding. It has also conveyed to its adversaries that the United States will not countenance rogue regimes nor tolerate economic aggression and unfair trade practices, and this is visible in its National Security Strategy document. For a country like India, this change in American policy works fine as we have neither been an ally that has disappointed nor have we been an adversary that has offended. In fact, the more America becomes bilateral, the more it will fit into India's preferred way of dealing with them.

As for Russia, we have witnessed a reversal of roles between China and Russia. In the old days, in Eurasia, China was the swing power—when China went towards the West it strategically damaged the Soviet Union—but today, Russia is the swing power. From our point of view, the events of the last few years have not been helpful as our interests do not dictate the kind of pressure that America is putting on Russia. However, the India-Russia relationship remains one of the dependable factors of our foreign policy. The other power that merits mention is Japan. We have seen a big change in terms of political closeness and Japanese investments and presence going up very sharply. However, impending systemic changes are still unfolding in Japan.

Despite bilateral relations becoming more popular, we should not underestimate the power of multilateralism. The coalition of support that we saw in the International Court of Justice elections was a result of multilateralism and can easily be termed as an election of the old order versus the new order. In the foreign policy business there are two attributes that should be prized more than anything else—between people it is chemistry, between nation's it is credibility. To be a power, leaders must build the chemistry and the country must have credibility. Moreover, we should continue to be ethical and follow international norms and rules. When others think of us, these attributes must come out clearly.

# 9

## Challenges and Opportunities

*V K Singh*

This paper discusses a few issues of India's foreign policy, broadly touching upon each region and how we look at it. A country's foreign policy, once developed, rarely changes but does undergo tweaking to obtain specific objectives. Like the national security policy which is based on everything that impacts the security of our nation, India's foreign policy is based on everything that affects its relations outside the country. It is multi-faceted and includes almost every facet that can impact a nations well-being. Within its ambit falls economics, energy, environment, people-to-people relations, diplomatic leverage to attain a particular objective, et al. All that forms part of the rubric of foreign policy.

Indian foreign policy since 2014 has been focussed on three specific objectives:

- Rejuvenating our relations with some of the areas which probably had not been given the requisite amount of attention earlier.
- Looking into measures that would make foreign policy more sensitive to the requirements of the nation.
- Looking into and adequately addressing economic concerns, when dealing with other nations.

Since 2014, a great deal of attention has been paid to extending India's outreach to all nations, which should have been done much earlier. Some of the nations visited by the Prime Minister had not been visited by a head of state for 30 years and many had not been visited for decades. It is important to reach out to other nations, because nations are much akin to individual society. If you do not meet your neighbour in the next house, you will never get to know about him. And if you go to that house and ask for assistance, they may well say, 'Who are you?' Nations too are similar. If we do not reach out and if we do not visit each other and maintain continuous contact, then relations will suffer. This is what I observed when I visited Venezuela. There were issues of concern to us and a ministerial level meeting was taking place after a very long time. However, all the issues were resolved through meeting people. Consequently, obstacles were removed and we found that there was nothing that could not be done between Venezuela and India.

This contact is what matters and that is why you will find that a large number of visits at ministerial level and at the level of the Prime Minister, Vice President and President have been undertaken so that we can reach out to each and every country.

While we have extended this outreach to most countries, a few are yet to be covered and we are sanguine that eventually we will extend this outreach to those countries as well. Similarly, attention has been given to some of the very small nations, who tend to get neglected. It must be remembered that all nations have one vote in the UN and that goes for small nations too. Small nations therefore are crucial to India and we expend a lot of energy in ensuring that we reach out to everybody. That is why we held the India-Pacific Islands Sustainable Development Conference in Suva, Fiji in May 2017, to enhance cooperation between India and Pacific Island Countries. Such a conference had never been done earlier, and it provided the platform for mutual sharing of concerns on the environment and climate change, and for better cooperation between the Island countries and India. This type of outreach has been very successful in enhancing cooperation and for getting support for Indian initiatives in the World body from the community of nations.

Sensitivity is another important issue. Earlier, when Indian nationals who got into trouble while abroad got little or no assistance from our missions, and if relief was provided it was generally not timely. The response mechanism was archaic and elitist, and a common citizen who was working abroad found it difficult to approach our embassy in that country. This has dramatically changed. The fact that in the last two and a half years, more than 90,000 people have been rescued and brought back to India, is a figure that speaks for itself.

Our embassies have been able to gain the confidence of the Indian people who are now assured that if they approach the embassy, they will be given the requisite assistance. There is however still some hesitancy and people resort to tweeting on the issue. When we ask them if they have approached our embassy there, they say they have not. We encourage them to approach the Embassy, and when they do, invariably their problems are taken care of. One of the functions of our embassies is to ensure that citizens who work abroad are taken care of and this sensitivity has now been brought in.

The third key issue is the pursuance of an economic agenda. No country, whether developed or developing can survive with a weak economy. It depends not only on the domestic market economy, but also on the balance of trade in terms of imports and exports and on what needs to be done for an assured supply of energy. It also encompasses ensuring that there is a free flow of trade and commerce between nations and that there are no disruptions.

While the above is the focus area of various ministries such as the Ministry of Commerce and Industry and others, the Ministry of External Affairs plays a very important role in ensuring that our missions are able to pursue India's economic agenda in the countries in which they are based. It is our missions abroad that are able to establish people to people contact, and look at issues which are related to commerce and trade. They can give guidance and advice back home on what action needs to be taken on a specific issue that will be advantageous to us. This would substantially improve India's overall economic health. These three factors then, have been the cornerstone in terms of tweaking of the foreign policy in the last three and a half years.

We have also reinvigorated our overseas Indian Affairs Department. Earlier, we had the Ministry of Overseas Indian Affairs. It was formed at a particular time to give prominence and importance to the people who go abroad and people who work abroad, to settle problems and issues related with what they were doing. As such, we had two different ministries working on the same subject, which created a certain amount of stovepipes syndrome. The embassies and missions and the consulates required a great amount of harmony between the two government systems. They have different levels of talking to each other and the level of coordination achieved would depend on the type of people who manned these offices. There were issues of coordination, despite the fact that when the present government came into being, the Minister for Ministry of Overseas Indian Affairs was the external affairs minister, to ensure better coordination. Minister of State for that ministry was also Minister of State in the external affairs ministry. Yet we found that there were problems and therefore we decided to merge the Ministry of Overseas Indian Affairs and make it a part of the external affairs ministry. A secretary level officer has been posted and we now have better coordination, a better relationship and better synergy in ensuring that overseas Indian Affairs can get the full support of all our missions. This has been one of the key changes that has helped us ensure that we are able to reach out to our people. It is this outreach that enabled us to bring back 90,000 of our people from disturbed areas abroad.

Overseas Indian Affairs is a major part of the work of the Ministry of External Affairs and we found with experience, that it needed to be part and parcel of the Ministry. We have many issues that come up in terms of various corporations, whether it is economic or security related and all these focus on policy issues and how such policies are to be pursued by our missions. All India missions abroad thus have a very important role to play in ensuring that our relationship remains on an even keel, that our economic agenda gets due boost and that we are able to take care of our diaspora, which indeed is a very large one. Our missions are also important in terms of giving accurate feedback and to recommend changes or alterations, if needed, so that necessary changes are done based on that. This sums up what India's foreign policy in the last three and a half years has been.

We have been able to ensure that our energy basket is well spread out and have been able to address problems that existed in trade and commerce. We have also pursued and taken care of free trade agreements where needed, and have been successful in projecting the economic viability of investing in India, which has led to a larger foreign direct investment. A country which is projected to be a bright spot in the world where economy is concerned needs the economic engine that we pushed for.

# ECONOMY AND SOFT POWER

# 10

## Economy as a Global Calling Card

*Suresh Prabhu*

The world is full of conflicts and tensions today. If everything would function smoothly and all the nations of the world lived peacefully with each other, there perhaps would be no need for diplomacy and diplomats. But friction and confrontation do exist in almost all parts of the world, which perforce dictates the need for diplomacy. We have diplomacy to prevent differences from degenerating into war, and during war we have diplomacy to provide a second channel between the warring parties. But the major driving force for diplomacy today is the promotion of international economic relations.

Foreign policy of any country is essentially required to promote a nation's domestic agenda. It's an extension of a country's domestic concerns articulated in terms of international relations in foreign policy. Both domestic and foreign policies have to be in sync with each other, if the domestic agenda is to be promoted and taken forward. And for all nations, the prime domestic agenda is and always will be economic growth, except perhaps in times of war when the demands are different. Therefore, essentially, a country's foreign policy has a very large component of its economic policy and is designed to create favourable conditions for the domestic environment.

India is a fast growing economy, with high rates of growth. The US economy, which is the world's largest economy, is by contrast growing at just above 2 per cent. But given the size of the US economy, even growth at this level creates a huge output. The Chinese economy too has slowed down after decades of above 10 per cent growth and is plateauing. India's economy will however continue to maintain a high rate of growth, at least for the foreseeable future. Despite the fact that India has a 2.5 trillion dollar economy, the challenges the country faces are enormous. A large part of the population is living below the poverty line, infrastructure needs are enormous and social sector development is required in a big way. This dictates the need for a fast growing economy, to enable an improvement in the living standards of its people. India thus has both the potential to grow as well as the need to grow. But we cannot grow in modern times at a faster rate unless we are integrated into the global economy. Prime Minister Narendra Modi spoke of this when he addressed the 48th World Economic Summit in Davos in January 2018, stating that India is for globalisation and that we want to engage with the rest of the world to promote global economic growth. He called for the world to invest in India and said that this was a part of India's Foreign Policy. India's main thrust therefore is for a diplomatic push to develop economic relationships to bring in faster economic growth in India.

India will grow by 2-3 per cent, more than the present number. We will also cross the mental barrier of 10 per cent growth and will continue to grow at that rate for the next two decades or more. That will prove to be the real game changer, because then the growth rate will be more than the aspirational rate of the people. And therefore, we will be able to match and create infrastructure, also at a matching rate. We have put in place the requisite domestic policies to facilitate this growth, but unless we get foreign investment into India to supplement our domestic savings, which fortunately are now on the rise, we will not be able to get the desired result because economic growth is a function of investment as well. The other side which makes economic growth possible is consumption, but investment remains the prime driving force. Economic output GDP cannot be achieved without appropriate inputs and these come from domestic savings and foreign direct investment. Even if domestic savings rise to much higher levels, we still need the rest of the world and our economic diplomacy has to be attuned to that possibility.

We also should be able to export more of our products. All the countries in the world which have registered phenomenal growth rate, whether it be China, Italy, Japan or Korea, have done so because they were integrated to the global grid in a big way. China is today the largest exporter and importer and also the largest manufacturer. They created the export market through manufacturing and getting access to global markets. If we do not get access to global markets we will not be able to sell our products, which in turn will affect our GDP. And with a low GDP, we will not be able to reduce poverty and bring affluence to the people of India.

The above simply means that India needs a policy to increase exports and we are working towards that end to enable India to have a five trillion dollar economy within the next seven to eight years with the present rate of growth. At least 40 per cent of that should come from global trade, both imports and exports and our economic diplomacy or foreign policy must be ready to make that happen. We must engage with countries that are going to export more, must get market access and we must develop a relationship at political level to facilitate exports. To make that happens we are putting a roadmap in place, of the products that India can export and how our foreign policy can be an enabler. This policy framework is being designed in consultation with the Foreign Minister.

There are two components or elements to this framework. The first is bilateral relationships. Here, we have some countries where India has invested a lot in terms of political capital and in some cases, even financial resources as well. Logically, where we have good political relations, the economic relationship should also be sound. But we have found that in many cases, despite excellent political relations, the economic relationship remains weak. Cuba is one such example. On my visit to Havana, therefore, I met all the top leadership and they all said that they would be happy to establish a sound economic relationship too. This means that where we have political goodwill, we need to convert that into good economic relations too. Conversely, where we see a potential of economic relations, but do not have a good political relationship, then our foreign policy interventions should seek to enhance and improve the political relationship so that the economic relationship can be developed. Here, we would need to go in for a bilateral contract or agreement and develop a long-term relationship, which will provide market access for our products as well as enable that country to export its products to India. Economic diplomacy must be premised on a win-win formula to make it sustainable.

The second element is to use multi-platforms to develop economic relationships, so that we get greater market access. In terms of multilateral strategies, at the WTO or on any other forum, India has to articulate the concerns of the poor, as she has a very large number of poor—perhaps the largest in the world. India is also one of the largest economies in the world, so she needs to focus on multilateral negotiations to ensure that the WTO remains relevant to modern times. India's foreign policy must thus be geared to seek trade openings where the political relationship is good. Where the political relationship is weak, it must seek to improve the relationship wherever there is potential for economic cooperation. It must also focus on multilateral engagements to further India's economic agenda.

India is also a very large service economy, with two-thirds of India's GDP coming from services. As India moves to a five trillion dollar economy, of which 40 per cent will be global trade, services will play a key role in exports, rising at a faster rate than merchandise exports. India thus needs to see how it can get access to services, which provide manifold advantages. Export of merchandise may lead to shortages within the country. When we export agricultural products, we are doing so at the cost of the limited quantity of water that we have. But when we export services, we export talent. Services also create more jobs than manufacturing as more jobs are created downstream within the country. This is what India needs to exploit and look at service sectors that have not yet been thought off. As an example, it could look into home care, where the elderly are provided comfort through audio and video conversations.

The principle idea behind economic diplomacy should be to get investments into the country, which will promote domestic growth. Technology must be embedded into economic diplomacy, to facilitate promotion of exports, which would include services, merchandise as well as agricultural products. Economic diplomacy also helps in geopolitical issues. Exports create an economic footprint in that country because somebody is importing, who then becomes a stakeholder. We thus create a huge pool of people from the two countries who get to know each other through economic activity. And when this goodwill gets expanded, it leads to political dividends.

Countries are more than willing to talk only about commerce and industry or economic activity than anything else. This point got highlighted when I visited Abu Dhabi for a high level task force meeting with three major foreign wealth fund investors, the Chair of the meeting being the brother of the crown prince of Abu Dhabi. The wealth of the foreign investors is rumoured to be in the range of two trillion dollars which is about the size of India's GDP. For a small population, there is thus an investible surplus, which makes India an attractive destination. They expressed interest in aligning their investment activity to the Indian vision, based on a 20–25 years investment strategy. There will be both economic benefits and geopolitical benefit. Across the world, leaders are talking about commerce and industry and so is India's Prime Minister as he wants to promote India's economy. This highlights the fact that diplomacy will increasingly be driven by economic considerations—A global calling card. India will remain an attractive destination as within 7-8 years it will be a 5 trillion dollar economy. In real terms, it means that we will be adding another India in just eight years, and that is the potential of India.

It will thus benefit investors to engage with India and that in turn will help us grow faster. India's calling card should therefore be its domestic economy. Primarily, we must understand that whatever we get is to further our domestic interest, while also benefitting the investor—A win-win situation. That is the model that we have to develop. That is why we have removed virtually all the caps on investment and all roadblocks too are being removed. And if India plays its cards right, it will be the biggest beneficiary of today's difficult world. The American economy is at a plateau, and with growing protectionism, it would make it that much more difficult for the US to engage with the rest of the world. In the EU, the driver of that big block is Germany, but there will be issues with Brexit. The Chinese economy too is slowing and India can benefit from this global situation. Our diplomacy should accordingly be designed to benefit from this already created geopolitical situation in which economic possibilities are enormous.

With a growing market, investors can be rewarded, especially as GST (Goods and Services Tax) and demonetisation have formalised our economy in a big way and this will give huge dividends in the future. The slight slowdown is the initial pain of reform, but it is temporary and growth is picking up now just as the pain is disappearing. We can look forward to faster growth in 2018 than in the previous year and an even higher rate of growth in 2019. That is the intrinsic strength of the economic potential of India. And that is why we need to align our diplomacy to achieve this goal of creating huge economic potential for us and others. The Indian market is not saturated, which provides an investment opportunity. There are difficulties, but these are being addressed, which has resulted in India's improved ranking in the ease of doing business. We also need to use international relations as a means of growing India's economy. China did that because they realised the importance of engaging with global community to foster economic growth in their own country. This is what India is now trying to do. Not because somebody else has done it but because this is the best strategy for India. This is India's global calling card. Our domestic economy is a calling card. Our prime minister is one of the most respected and most sought-after global leaders in the world today. In Davos, at least 60 heads of state were present, but Prime Minister Modi got the honour to introduce the plenary session. The leadership of India's Prime Minister too is India's calling card. I think we should capitalise on it and make the best of it.

# 11

## Economic Reforms: Shared Prosperity and Changing the Architecture

*Shaurya Doval*

India is a $2.5 trillion economy that is growing by 7–10 per cent a year. It is the seventh largest economy in the world in nominal terms. It took India 60 years after independence to become a $1 trillion economy, but thereafter, it took just seven years to add the second trillion to the economy (GDP at current prices). India is expected to become a $3 trillion economy by 2019–20 and a $4 trillion economy by 2024. In terms of global wealth creation, India's economic figures are doing what continents do. The other dimension to the Indian economy is that India is still a poor country. Our GDP per capita is $1600 and this reflects in our rankings. Interestingly, both these facts continue to exist in parallel and the irony is that both are true. Therefore, it will require a lot of time and effort to make a difference to the lives of Indians and we must be aware while talking about the Indian economy that this is not a normal economy.

It is in this context that the new government under Prime Minister Modi was elected. To understand the Prime Minister's reforms we need to understand "shared economy"—creating prosperity and sharing it. The contours of Prime Minister Modi's economic reforms point to a few trends. First, there is a breakout trend. It is for the first time that India has started to think big about what it wants to achieve. The Prime Minister's Make in India, 'Jan Dhan Yojana' and Smart Cities are all big and ambitious projects.

Second, this government is following a two-pronged approach, a top-down approach along with a bottom-up approach. The latter approach emphasises inclusiveness while the former emphasises policies that accelerate growth through shared prosperity. Other elements of the top-down approach include unlocking state-controlled resources such as coal, oil and gas and telecom spectrum allocation where the government raised $330 billion, $40 billion and $26 billion respectively.

Third, we recognise that we cannot accelerate growth without attracting investment. The dividends of the Prime Minister's push to attract foreign investment are visible today—we are the largest receivers of FDI having doubled from approximately $30 billion four years ago to $65 billion today. Fourth, India introduced GST to create a common tax net. This progressive tax system is destination based, multistage and on value addition. Keeping aside the teething problems, GST alone will add $250 to $500 billion in incremental GDP and 1.5 per cent to 2 per cent increase in GDP per year. More importantly, it will reduce production costs by 10 per cent. In the Indian context, these are very large numbers.

Fifth, an increase in GDP will not necessarily result in shared prosperity unless we create employment. The manufacturing sector can alone absorb a million people every month into the workforce but accounts for only 16 per cent of India's GDP. Economists suggest we need to increase this to 25–30 per cent of our GDP to add hundred million jobs over the course of the next five years. Unfortunately, we have not been able to reach these goals but the government has pushed for a growth in the sector through Make in India and indigenous defence procurement. Yet, constraints like cost of capital, skilled manpower and innovation remain.

Sixth, the government has focused tremendously on the fight against corruption through demonetisation, renegotiation of tax treaties with tax havens, Black Money Imposition Tax Act 2015 and Income Declaration Schemes. Corruption is a long-haul social fight, but fighting corruption will contribute to the growth of our economy as the economy pays a huge price in terms of innovation and crowds out talent due to corruption. It is estimated that 25 per cent of India's GDP is in the black economy. When "black money" comes back into the system it can be used for more productive purposes to boost the economy. Therefore, tackling corruption will play a role in helping India transition from a $3 trillion economy to a $4 trillion economy.

Seventh, one of the biggest challenges that prohibits India from becoming a globally competitive economy is that cost of capital is very high, making it difficult for the Indian entrepreneur to become globally competitive. Therefore, reforming the banking sector is necessary to lower the cost. In the next three to four years we will be able to see the impact of the changes in the banking sector. The progress that India has achieved in the last four years is unprecedented.

These initiatives will allow greater wealth to be created. More importantly, it will allow for shared prosperity as one cannot have islands of prosperity in a sea of poverty. Lack of shared prosperity leads to violence and Maoism. In 2011, out of 250 million households, 145 million had access to banking. In rural areas out of 170 million households, 90 million had access while in urban areas out of 80 million households, 53 million had access. From 2014 to 2018, 308 million bank accounts had been opened of which 180 million were in rural areas and 126 million in urban areas, which is more than what India achieved in the first 65 years of independence. Moreover, 90 per cent of the newly opened bank accounts are being used and 232 million RuPay debit cards were issued. With opening of these accounts, benefits can be directly transferred to the weaker sections of society, saving the government about Rs 57,000 crore. Unsurprisingly, the number of beneficiaries also increased from 10 crore to 65 crore.

Therefore, when India transitions into its 75th or 100th year, it will not be a small transition but will be a transition that will swing the entire GDP of the world. The question now remains that when this prosperity comes will India have the receiving systems or the architecture to allow the prosperity to be fairly distributed? The Soviet Union is a classic example of a country that could not absorb the benefits of opening up. In conclusion, to fully understand the economic reforms over the last four years we must consider the two terms—"shared prosperity" and "changing India's economic architecture."

# 12

## Soft Power and Foreign Policy

*David Frawley*

Soft power is one of the key components of foreign policy in this age of mass communication, global trade and tourism. This soft power includes cultural factors, sharing the intellectual, artistic and spiritual culture of a country with the other nations of the world. Soft power is part of what we can perhaps better call "cultural diplomacy," using culture to create a favourable foreign policy image for a country to expand its associations and its interests. Cultural diplomacy aids in educating the people of foreign countries as to the values and heritage of a nation, and can correct negative portrayals in foreign media, academic and political presentations.

In this multicultural world today, there is a clear and pronounced clash of cultures. If a country today does not communicate and promote its own culture to the world at large, then its culture may be undermined, undervalued or lose credibility even at home. When a country loses its cultural identity, other national interests may come under threat. Cultural diplomacy thus has many economic, political and social benefits, and also aids in the defence and security of a nation.

Such cultural diplomacy is particularly important in the case of India that is one of the world's oldest, most profound and diverse civilisations, with an enduring worldwide impact. India's older civilisational connections with the many countries of Southeast Asia form a common cultural heritage that can aid in favourable relationships and sustain a common regional identity. India can benefit from such cultural alliances with its neighbours, and they too can benefit from having India as a cultural ally to help sustain their own national ethos from inimical outside forces.

Extending to East Asia that has adopted India's 'Dharmic' traditions for many centuries, cultural diplomacy can aid in communication, common values and overcoming clashing national interests for a broader regional consensus. At a global level, India's ancient culture of tolerance, diversity and peace can be a model for creating harmony between competing nations and the different clashing cultures, ancient and modern, of the entire world.

Humanity should strive to preserve the unique cultural heritages of different countries and regions, not simply reduce them to a uniform model in the global arena. This is much like the ecological need to preserve biodiversity. Cultural diversity is under threat in many areas of the world, where languages and local cultures are quickly disappearing with rapid urbanisation. This is particularly true in India where many local and tribal cultures are struggling to survive.

Exporting culture, however, requires that the culture within the country is supported as well. If local cultural traditions are not maintained, there will be little of any unique culture to export to the outside. Yet cultural diplomacy also gives value and prestige to the native cultures within the country, particularly when it enables cultural leaders and groups to travel, teach and perform throughout the world.

India's potential soft power and cultural diplomacy is reflected in its vast and unique heritage that is already influencing the world by its own intrinsic value. This is indicated by the worldwide popularity of India's Yogic teachings and Dharmic traditions that historically have been centred in India. This process should be supported in the light of cultural diplomacy.

## India's Civilisational Strength

India has a tremendous cultural and civilisational power that has maintained a profound impact on the world for thousands of years. This is most clearly represented by India's great gurus, yogis and Dharmic traditions at an inner level, along with a sophisticated intellectual, artistic and material culture outwardly. India's many-sided civilisation spread to Indochina and Indonesia from the start of their histories and their formative period of development. It had a profound and lasting influence on China, Japan and East Asia, becoming an integral to their own civilisational identities as part of a greater sphere of

Dharmic civilisation. Such historical ties are of great relevance today when Asia is seeking to awaken and reclaim its identity and prestige.

Since the dawn of civilisation, India has maintained regular trade contacts with Mesopotamia and the Middle East. India's connections with ancient Iran by language and religion are well known, with the two cultures closely intertwined at many points of time. India's civilisation was honoured in ancient Greece and Rome on intellectual, spiritual and economic levels. Indo-European traditions that dominated ancient Europe like the Celts, Germans and Slavs had much in common with India's older Vedic culture. India had a significant influence on Central Asia through Afghanistan, which for many centuries was part of an Indic and Buddhist cultural sphere, including the Silk Trail. India's maritime influence along the Spice Trail brought many cultural influences through the Indo-Pacific region as well.

Such Indian civilisational influences flourished from ancient periods up to the Islamic era starting in the eighth century, when these began to decline; a decline that increased during the colonial era when the British suppressed India's native culture and its extensive networks of trade and communication, supplanting them with its own. Yet, while India's civilisational influence declined, it did persist. India's science and medicine reached the Islamic world, like the Arab adaptation of India's decimal system starting in the ninth century. From the eighteenth century, western thinkers came into contact with Hindu and Buddhist thought. One can mention such notable figures as Voltaire, Goethe, Schopenhauer, Emerson and Thoreau among those who expressed their admiration for India.

## Modern Yoga and India's Soft Power

It was Swami Vivekananda's travels to the West starting in 1893 that ignited a major resurgence of India's cultural influences throughout the world, led by a global adaptation of Yoga-based teachings and practices. Vivekananda's emphasis on universal consciousness and self-realisation paralleled the work of Einstein in breaking down time and space barriers and ushering in a new unitary vision of the cosmos. Vivekananda was also one of the primary inspirations in India's national awakening that motivated India's independence movement. His work of spreading Yoga to the West was complemented by his restoring respect within the country for its own Dharmic traditions, which were dismissed as regressive under foreign rule.

## The Global Yoga and Dharma Movement

The world Yoga movement continued to expand exponentially throughout the 20th century. A major upsurge of interest in Yoga and meditation occurred in the West in the 1960s, with a steady growth since. Numerous Indian gurus have travelled throughout the world teaching Yoga and meditation, with Tibetan teachers often joining them. Today, perhaps over a hundred million people throughout the world practice some form of Yoga. Though asanas remain the main focus, pranayama, mantra and meditation are often included.

Yoga training programs routinely examine traditional Yoga texts like the Yoga Sutras and Bhagavad Gita. Many Yoga students follow gurus and lineages from India and take on Sanskrit names. Great gurus like Paramhansa Yogananda, Ramana Maharshi, Sri Aurobindo, Maharishi Mahesh Yogi, Satya Sai Baba, Sri Sri Ravi Shankar, Mata Amritananda-mayi, Sadhguru Jaggi Vasudev, and many others have become recognisable names in numerous countries. For their students, Yoga is not just a fitness system but a complete culture and way of life. Yoga has brought with it important aspects of Indian culture including Sanskrit mantras, Hindu kirtans, Indian music and dance, pujas and yajnas, and a new orientation towards Vedic sciences. Remarkably, ancient Ayurveda has emerged as one of the cutting edge forms of mind-body medicine in the world today. The study of Sanskrit at a popular level in the world has increased rapidly.

## Independent India's Failure to Develop its Soft Power

During this extraordinary spread of India's cultural traditions through the 20th century, the government of independent India did little to encourage or to benefit from it. Perhaps no other country in recent times has so ignored the potential value of its soft power and so much neglected the role of cultural diplomacy. Even China, whose culture the Communist Cultural Revolution not long ago tried to eradicate, is now happy to promote its traditional medicine and martial arts, along with Chinese art, dance and commerce.

India's leftist academia has been happier denigrating the country's older culture, than producing any deeper scholarship that worldwide friends of India can appreciate. India's Congress party rule showed some respect for Yoga, particularly under Indira Gandhi, but did little to actually support Yoga nationally or internationally.

## New India and its New Vision of Yoga

The present BJP government is the first to truly honour India's soft power and proudly share it. The Modi government has emphasised India's cultural gifts to the world, and aimed to strengthen diplomatic connections, particularly with the countries of Asia most influenced by India in the past. Cultural power must form an integral part of any realistic foreign policy.

Narendra Modi's new Yoga initiative, starting with International Yoga Day, is a welcome break from India's prior cultural lethargy. It marks a new era, a new India that honours its millennial civilisation and strives to share it. His government is introducing Yoga training into the schools, not limiting Yoga to exercise but including Yoga philosophy and meditation. Modi's new India is a rebirth of yogic India from its classical era of world influence.

Indian Council of Cultural Relations (ICCR) can play an important role in this new expression of soft power and cultural diplomacy. ICCR has the facilities and associations in the many countries of the world that are necessary to enable it. It is imperative that India expands its soft power and civilisational strength, both for national unity and to gain the proper place in the world for its magnificent heritage that can benefit all humanity. India has the cultural and civilisational depth to lead the world to a new era of peace and higher consciousness, but needs the political will and the diplomatic skill in order to do so. Developing that is essential and should not be neglected. It requires a new generation of seasoned diplomats with a worldview in harmony with India's civilisational values.

# 13

## Winning Hearts and Minds

*Vinay Sahasrabuddhe*

One can read the intellectually stimulating works of Joseph Nye to understand soft power that emerged after World War II when people realised that wars are not going to take us too far in our attempt to establish a supremacy of a nation. Yet wars continue to occur, although their magnitude has reduced and the victories and limitations of war were underscored in the developments of World War II. Soft power was thereafter looked at as an alternative.

To trace the history of soft power, especially in India, we can look back at the 15th century when King Zamorin of Kerala welcomed Vasco da Gama. This was perhaps the first manifestation of India's soft power, having established India as a confluence of civilisations and worship. People across the world wanted to visit India and experience India from Columbus to Vasco da Gama. Alternatively, the Indian ideology of 'Vasudeva Kutumbakam' (The world is one family) also highlights India's soft power, by saying the world is one. We provided shelter to Tibetans and Bangladeshis who had come to India. This was not necessary diplomacy, but is rather deep rooted in our culture itself.

India's soft power diplomacy perhaps became official through the establishment of the Indian Council for Cultural Relations (ICCR). ICCR offers scholarships to students to study in India, conducts teacher exchanges, hosts cultural programs and organises festivals of India across the world, among other activities. The festivals of India for example, are events that showcase India's rich culture through dance, music and even folk activities. However, the agenda of ICCR should not be confined to only these activities.

Soft power tries to influence the opinions of the world. It requires opinion makers like politicians, filmmakers and artists to fully understand India, before they can change the opinions of others. India is not a country that can be understood by reading books or visiting a website. To truly understand India, one must visit India. I recall an incident when I was sitting on a train in Berlin, reading a Hindi newspaper, when a co-passenger asked me if I was an Indian. The passenger went on to explain that he made the guess as he recognised the Hindi script from his visit to India. When I asked him his opinion of India, he said it is a massive country, with many people—an extremely crowded country with garbage strewn everywhere and some amount of lawlessness as people easily break traffic rules. He then told me that he extended his stay in India! Why, I asked? "Because" he replied, "in spite of all these factors, Indians are very lively people, and the glitter you see in their eyes, is not something he ever experienced outside India."

Therefore, people must come to India to experience India. To give another example, Bill Clinton had visited India for the first time when he was President of the US. There was a marked change in his approach to India after his visit—after he experienced India. The same was true of President Obama—there was more warmth and keenness to have a closer relationship with India. The fact remains that for India's soft power to be further evolved, to provide a sound foundation for our diplomatic and economic relationships, this people-to-people connection needs to be strengthened. It needs to be understood that India as an idea needs to be tested. Until people visit India, and experience it, India faces an uphill task in educating people, as around the world, there is a lot of ignorance regarding India. I recently met a lady from Moscow who has visited India, especially Maharashtra, many times. She tells me that even today, in Moscow, the idea of India doesn't move beyond the land of snake charmers, cattle on the street, Mahatma Gandhi and Raj Kapoor.

ICCR is thinking of undertaking a project in several countries where we will examine the textbooks that are being taught in those countries. We want to know whether those lessons are helping enhance India's literacy or if those lessons are contributing to more misperceptions. It is necessary to review the differences on India from different textbooks to understand what has gone wrong and why. We need to work overtime to dispel many wrong conceptions about India and we need to project the transformations that are underway in the country. India needs to overcome this perception deficit for it to exert its soft power.

Through various cultural presentations that ICCR makes internationally, we need to ensure to incorporate the peripheral sections of India. Indian dance, for example, is not confined to Bharatanatyam and Kuchipudi. There are Kodagu and Arunachal tribals, for example, who also need to be given an opportunity to showcase their art on an international platform. Even Indian cuisine is extremely diverse but is not showcased worldwide. India's soft power strategy needs to be made comprehensive and inclusive for us to enhance the idea of India even for people who have not experienced the country.

Soft power is also important for our foreign policy. Unlike hard power, soft power requires efforts but is not costly. Asserting our nation through soft power requires a silent and unobtrusive strategy and unlike hard power, soft power need not be dependent on the government. Herein lies the importance of people-to-people connect. However, soft power requires more time, but it is also more enduring. In the Indian context, if all the relevant departments in the government join hands, then we can effectively provide a sound structure to build our economic power and diplomatic base as well, for which the foundation must be laid on soft power. It is hard to say whether India will become a military or economic superpower, but as an Indian and a student of Indian polity, I can certainly say that the strength of Indian soft power is so strong that India can easily win hearts and make inroads in the minds of people that matter.

# 14

## Soft Power and Diplomacy

*Veena Sikri*

Soft power is a comprehensive rubric that includes civilisational heritage and traditional knowledge, language, literature, philosophy (including religions), education and academia, culture, cuisine, yoga, tourism, and contemporary life-styles, embracing in its ambit the 21st century usage of social media through the internet. Taking all these aspects into account, India's soft-power strengths are legion, outdoing almost every other country.

India's soft power should be looked at through the lens of achieving our foreign policy objectives. India's soft power has taken on a new role in the last three years with the Prime Minister's visits abroad and also with leaders of the world visiting India. In both contexts, Shri Narendra Modi has given soft power an unprecedented importance in India's foreign policy. He has used soft power to highlight India's achievements and has succinctly leveraged India's soft power as an important tool for realising its foreign policy goals.

Soft power projection through diplomacy involves harnessing India's cultural and civilisational heritage to augment the country's strength on the global stage. There is also smart and sharp power, but these differ from soft power as they include economic and military strength. After World War II, the concept of soft power came into its own when governments realised the value of shaping the ideas of others, especially through the media. Governments and their agencies played a dominant role in this process. The 21st-century cyber age has seen the democratisation of this power over opinion, especially through social media. With the cyber revolution, the vitality of people-to-people diplomacy is inescapable. It is no longer enough to focus just on convincing other governments, or a handful of influential opinion-makers, be they from academia, the media or even the corporate world. The canvas is much wider than ever before, and the power of popular opinion cannot be brushed aside or ignored. Today, public opinion is no longer just the measure of power but also the source of power.[1]

The enormously diverse and multiple dimensions of India's soft power offer a unique opportunity, provided that the utilisation of this soft power through public diplomacy channels can be effectively integrated as part of the foreign policy armoury. In recent years, soft-power diplomacy has been deftly practised by India's leaders. Yet the Indian system, including its diplomatic structure, still has to fully recognise soft-power diplomacy as an integral pillar of its own foreign policy objectives. Such recognition is vital in order to achieve success.

How does India project its soft power outside its frontiers? A vital role is played by the work of institutions like ICCR (Indian Council for Cultural Relations), in many ways the nodal agency for India's soft power diplomacy. Three significant areas of activity of ICCR relate to India's cultural centres abroad; the numerous chairs of Indian studies in foreign universities; and a vast programme that each year brings several thousand foreign students to India to study in universities and cultural institutions. These three aspects combined represent the core of India's soft power projection efforts. Cultural centres help spread the knowledge and practice of Indian culture and also act as a focal point for those interested in Indian culture. These cultural centres should be able to integrate the projection of India's civilisational aspects with other more contemporary foreign policy objectives, be these economic or political. The activities of the cultural centres epitomise the people-to-people dimension of foreign policy. It is essential that the cultural centres have the expertise to manage this dimension by reaching out to people, building friendships, so that they understand and are convinced of India's achievements and its good intentions.

Students are vital, as the opinions and impressions formed during university years play an important role for the rest of their working lives. In most foreign universities, with a few striking exceptions, there is very little taught about India through the academic curriculum, or through India-centric activities. As a result, it is difficult to expect graduate students across the world to have a positive opinion about India, or to be sensitive to India's interests. For them, India is an entirely new experience and lack of knowledge about the country will inhibit them in viewing India as a good investment destination, or as a thought-leader in the world. This highlights the need to work actively with foreign universities, to integrate India studies into existing curriculum, across the wide cross-section of faculties.

Successful management of the large numbers of foreign students who come to India each year is critical. The foreign students who return to their respective countries with good academic credentials and positive experiences, are lifelong friends of India. ICCR has taken important steps to streamline the intake of foreign students, and to reverse some of the bitter experiences of the past. ICCR's cultural centres in Indian missions abroad should pay great attention to keeping in touch with foreign students who have returned after studying in India, to reinforce and follow up on their academic stay.

One key aspect necessary to ensure the success of soft-power diplomacy is coordination: within the Indian missions abroad, as well across departments within the Government of India. This also means building sound public-private partnerships, to integrate and bring on board the successes of the Indian film industry, and the outstanding role that Persons of Indian Origin (PIOs) and NRIs are playing in their respective countries of residence. Soft power projection requires a coordinated effort, brought together under the Ministry of External Affairs. Tourism is an example of a sector which is a huge revenue and employment generating industry, and plays a vital role in soft power projection. The interaction between soft power projection and economic objectives is significant, but reaping its full benefits requires extensive coordination between various ministries, and in missions abroad, between different officers and sections.

Success in digital diplomacy is a reflection of soft power projection. Prime Minister Modi is one of the most followed international leaders in the world, and with his example, many of the ministries have become digitally oriented. Finally, we need to be able to evaluate what we have done over the years, especially whether we have been able to use soft power effectively in achieving foreign policy objectives. Honest evaluation is vital for successful implementation.

## NOTE

[1]See Alan Henrikson, "What Can Public Diplomacy Achieve?" Netherlands Institute of International Relations Clingendael, 2006, p. 2.

# 15

## The Diaspora: Establishing a Civilisational Connect

*Vijay Chauthaiwale*

A unique aspect of Prime Minister Narendra Modi's foreign policy initiatives has been not just his interaction with the diaspora, but in interacting with them on a massive scale. This started with his first trip to the US, where he attended more than 20 big and small programs and interacted with the diaspora. And he has done that repeatedly in all his foreign visits, which have been extensively covered on TV.

Are there any overarching principles behind all these initiatives? These are not done in isolation nor are these spur of the moment impulses, but are well thought out and planned, to build upon the civilisational connect, which in turn is a key component of India's foreign policy under the Modi government. And when it is seen in this context, its importance becomes self-evident. It is not only the big diaspora events like Madison Square Garden and Wembley which are important, but smaller events too, like the temple visit in Sri Lanka and Dhaka. Or the visit to China where Prime Minister Modi connected his hometown Vadnagar with a Chinese village where a terracotta culture existed several hundred years ago. When he went to Mauritius he went to Gangasagar, which is considered to be as pious and revered as the Ganga is in Bharat.

These are all the indicators of having a civilisational connect with persons of Indian origin, wherever such persons may be in the world, something that had not received due attention earlier. And with the establishment of that connect, such persons now view India as a home, along with their allegiance to their own country. This is not restricted to NRIs or Indian passport holders, but includes each and every person who has a connection with India, however remote that may be. In the course of the last three and half years, I have met many people who are actually natives of that country, who may be black or white or brown, but who very proudly show me their Overseas Citizens of India (OCI) card. They proudly say that one of their parents was of Indian origin and therefore they are now OCI and so have similar rights, affection and connection with India as anyone else. This is a very positive development for it shows an enormous amount of affection, not only towards their forefathers, but also towards the country. For example, the current Prime Minister of Portugal, António Luís Santos da Costa has roots which can be traced to India. His paternal grandfather, Luís Afonso Maria da Costa, was a Goan Catholic. In 2015, Prime Minister Narendra Modi presented the Overseas Citizen of India card to him, when he came to India as Chief Guest at the 14th Pravasi Bharatiya Diwas and described him as one of the best of the Indian diaspora across the world. The diaspora is thus of considerable importance to the country and can go a long way in improving relations between two countries.

It must be noted however, that the Indian diaspora is not uniform. Out of around 3 crore or so of the diaspora, around 1.5 crore are NRIs, and the rest are Persons of Indian Origin (PIO). If you go to places like Durban or Mauritius or Surinam, there are people who have been living there for 100-150 years. In Oman, there is a Kachchi Gujarati family from the last 150 years. They are still following their tradition but now have become so much integrated in the local society that the eldest in their family has been given the title of Sheikh by the Sultan of Oman. Many PIOs are from the lower middle class and some, especially in South Africa, live in very poor conditions, because of the earlier policy of apartheid. At the other end of the spectrum, there are people like Satya Nadella, who rose through the IT revolution and many others who have made a name for themselves who are big businessmen, doctors, entrepreneurs, world-class professors and renowned scientists. The Indian diaspora thus covers practically every part of society.

The Indian diaspora is also extremely fragmented. As in India, where we have differences based on religion, caste, creed, language and class, the same replica of miniaturised India is reflected in the diaspora. In London alone there are more than 1000 Indian organisations. In New York or even in the Bay Area, in the US, there are close to 500-600 Indian organisations each. To bring all of them together remains a major task for our embassies. What the policies of the Narendra Modi government have done is to bring them together and give them a larger identity in addition to their existing regional or linguistic identity. Because of this show of strength of the Indian diaspora, the local people have started taking note of the Indian diaspora and view it in a more positive light. For example, in Bay Area, Indian people were largely seen as behind the industrial rise through their contributions as IT specialists, business development and other contributions to the local economy. They were however seen on an individual basis and not as a collective force. But that has changed now. The Indian diaspora has now become important and their stature has gone up because of PM Modi. And they are being seen by the local community as a force, and in many cases, as a political force.

This impact is visible. When Prime Minister Modi went to Canada, the then President, Mr. Harper, accompanied him for the entire three-day programme, travelling with him in Air India One and also addressing the Indian diaspora along with Mr Modi. Similarly, in the UK, where over 60,000 people had gathered at Wembley to interact with Mr Modi, the then British Prime Minister, Mr David Cameron, was also present. Just a week prior to the event, when Mr Modi had met the British premier and formally invited him to the event, Mr Cameron told him that he had heard that 60,000 people would be at the event, but added that if he were to go to Wembley, he would find it difficult to fill the town hall, which had a capacity of just a thousand people! In Kenya, where Mr Modi addressed another gathering, the Kenyan President sent a message just three hours before the event that he too would like to come and address the gathering. World leaders are now seeing the Indian community as a potential political constituency, even if the community is very small. For example, in Canada, the Indian community constitutes barely 3 per cent of the voters, but is still considered significant. This is happening in the UK too. In the US Congress in 2017, five PIOs were elected to the US Congress, which is indicative of the fact that the Indian community is having an electoral impact.

These are some of the very visible changes on the domestic political front which are affected by diaspora. Many people in the US say that one of the reasons for President Trump's victory was the swing in the Indian votes towards him, which traditionally went to the Democrats. While this has not been independently verified, it is still an indication of the strength of the Indian diaspora in the local communities. This is a connection that was earlier lacking, but is being strengthened now.

But many ambiguities still exist, calling for a more effective outreach to the diaspora. New issues have now cropped up which did not exist earlier. For example, a lot of IT people, especially those who had spent over 10 years in the US, have now moved back to India. Their children were born in the US, and they are US citizens, holding US passports, but they are studying in India. The question arises that after their 12th standard exam, will they be eligible for getting admission in our medical colleges? And what will be their status? Will they be considered under the normal quota or under the NRI quota? Because of a lack of understanding, many applications for such admissions have been rejected. Similarly, if a person has studied in a CBSE school, say from Oman, can that person apply for an Indian medical school in the NRI quota? Such ambiguities need early resolution.

There are also issues about the OCI card. In Israel, there are around 80,000 Jews of Indian origin who reside in Israel. Even the Israeli government was not aware of such a large Indian origin community, till Prime Minister Modi went there. In Israel, military service is compulsory, but India has a law that those who have served in a foreign military cannot be given an OCI card. If this rule was implemented, then after one generation, there would be no OCI card holder in Israel, because practically everyone has to serve in the military. So a special dispensation was made for Israel, with Prime Minister Modi announcing that an exception had been made for Israel. The period of compulsory military service was not to be taken into account if the individual returned to a civilian job. Only in the event of the person continuing in the military after the period of compulsory service, would the person become ineligible to get the OCI card. Issues such as these will continue to crop up and will have to be handled in innovative ways.

Even the social media is being extensively made use of to assist Indians who require help. There was a rather humorous incident of a newly married couple who had bought their plane tickets for somewhere in Russia, planning to spend their honeymoon there when at the last moment they realised that the lady's passport had expired. All it took was a tweet to the External Affairs Minister, explaining their plight and the response was instantaneous. They were told to go to the local passport office where the passport would be issued in 24 hours and that is exactly what happened. This level of activism is unheard in any foreign policy regime, but is a part of the Indian system now, which has become highly sensitised to people's concerns. This was also reflected when an

Indian passenger in a Lufthansa flight from Frankfurt suffered a heart attack, necessitating the flight be diverted to Teheran. Assistance was immediately provided by the consulate, though it was unfortunate that the person could not survive. This goes to show the length to which the Indian government will go to assist the people, making them a part of the "parivar." The change in attitude in our embassies is visible, and is being appreciated. The focus on the diaspora is thus a positive development in the Indian foreign policy interventions.

# 16

## Significance of the Diaspora

*Dhyaneshwar Mulay*

For India, no foreign policy matter is really complete, without the mention of the Indian diaspora. This has been a major policy intervention since 2014, under the Narendra Modi led NDA government. Prior to this period, the diaspora was considered only in a peripheral manner. Now, it has become an important pillar of the ministry's work and its overall approach to the world.

In the address delivered by the President of India in early February 2018, he made mention of the Foreign policy initiatives of the government and highlighted the success achieved. Here, mention was made of the expansion of passport services, the successful evacuation of over 90,000 persons and the first ever Persons of Indian Origin (PIO) Parliamentarians Conference, that India hosted at the Pravasi Bharatiya Kendra (PBK) in New Delhi on the occasion of Pravasi Bhartiya Diwas (PBD) on 9 January 2018. All of these come under the Indian Overseas Affairs Division and the Consular, Passport and Visa (CPV) Division of the Ministry of External affairs. In essence, what was highlighted by the President was the new approach to the diaspora and that we need to know our own family and how big it is.

In terms of number, this larger family is over 31.2 million people. Of these, 17 million are the PIO and the rest are Non-Resident Indians (NRI). Numbers alone, however, do not reveal the full picture. When viewed in terms of the spread of this larger family and the positions that they occupy, the full extent of the significance of our diaspora comes to light. There are many countries where the diaspora exceeds 20 per cent of the local population and at any given point of time there are at least one to three heads of government or heads of state from the diaspora.

In a survey that we did two months prior to our PBD conference, we found out that there were 285 members of parliament sitting all over the world, in the parliaments of their respective countries. So essentially, this is a very strong asset that we have and we need to see how we can work with them in partnership to connect better as well as to facilitate better coordination and collaboration. This is primarily how we are approaching the issue of our diaspora. We look at them as an extension of the Indian family which is 125 crore plus people. We understand that they are spread out overseas and that we need to take care of our extended family.

The next element is working together on the maxim, 'help us to help you.' I think the India-US Civil Nuclear Agreement is an excellent example as to how the diaspora can work with the government to see that the bilateral relations could be strategically improved by collaborating with the diaspora. The third element is that in the present times, both domestic and external issues are intertwined. Domestic issues are no longer purely domestic and external issues are no longer purely external. Here, we refer to issues such as international marriages, trafficking, illegal agents and myriad other issues which may be external but become domestic. We care and if necessary we dare. These are the few elements that go into the decision-making process, though they are not defined anywhere. And we have coined specific slogans to cater to the needs of the diaspora.

We have grouped the diaspora into four specific components. I would deal first with the least privileged of our diaspora which is in the Gulf and which has 8.5 million people. This is a huge number and in many cases, it is more than the population of that country. We have to take care of these people because many of them are unskilled, semi-skilled or under-skilled. The next grouping is the PIO or the older diaspora. The third is the NRI plus, who have recently migrated and taken the citizenship of other countries, primarily in Europe, America and other developed countries. And the fourth group is the floating diaspora. Every person who goes abroad from India, whether it is a short-term visit or a stay for extended periods, becomes temporarily part of that diaspora and we have to take care of those people. And we have been doing that.

For the people residing in the Gulf, we have coined a slogan, 'Surakshit jao, prashikshit jao'. We have created an entire ecosystem to take care of their welfare, the protection under the local laws, the human rights. A look into the immigration portal of the MEA, gives out what all has been done here. When a labourer or a worker moves, from the time he signs the contract with his employer in the Gulf or with his agent in India, till the individual returns, we are now able to look after the person by putting in place everything that is required to enable the same.

The next slogan that we have coined is 'Videsh main aapka Dost, Bharatiya Dutavaas.' This slogan simply conveys the message to the diaspora that you have somebody to look after you when you go abroad and that is the Indian Embassy. Most people would have seen how assistance is being provided from the tweets of the External Affairs Minister or the work being done and reflected in evacuation of people trapped in areas where hostilities have begun. The underlying principle being followed is that Indians stranded and in distress anywhere in the world will be provided assistance. This is indeed a major development for any government and represents a big step forward. We have been able to do that and have not only sensitised all our embassies but have given them the role and have delegated powers to them as enablers, so that every problem that comes to them, irrespective of who the person is, so long as the person is an Indian citizen, the individual will be looked after. Towards that end, we have created an Indian community welfare fund which is at the disposal of our missions. They are now able to send the mortal remains, help someone in distress, or even feed people for a few days. This way, the embassy is able to save people from exploitation. People in prison are also contacted and mercy/clemency pleas are pursued. The aim is to provide help where needed. Besides the 90,000 people evacuated, over 110,000 people have been provided assistance in the last three years through the Indian community welfare fund. This by all accounts is a major achievement.

While working for the diaspora, we realise that not only the foreign governments but the state governments too are important stake holders. This is another major change in approach from the policies of the earlier governments. So we have now regular dialogue with the state governments too. The Minister for External Affairs has held six meetings with CMs and others from the state to tell them about the importance of these activities that we are doing and how important it is for us to cooperate with the state governments.

We also have something called Videsh Sampark Programme, where I go with my officers, and sometimes the Minister of State goes to engage with the local governments and other stakeholders, and inform them of the activities of the Foreign Ministry and how best they can take help from us. The other segments, viz. students, tourists, etc., are also taken care of. We have instructed our embassies and our consulates to be in touch with the students, who in turn are encouraged to register. Ambassadors now go to the universities and call the students to the embassies and hold regular receptions for them. Community organisations helping the students are also helped by the government to hold and conduct these activities and help them to be comfortable. As a result, we are now reasonably confident that things like what happened in Australia, between our students and the local authorities, will not be repeated and if something does happen, the embassy can step in quickly and intervene.

These are some of the major interventions that have happened since the present government took over. For those people who are not necessarily Indian citizens but are of Indian descent, we have the Overseas Citizens of India (OCI) card. This card is least understood, but put simply, it is a Green Card plus. It is a long-term visa. It enables buying property, establishing business and gaining employment in India. It also paves the way for taking Indian citizenship. It is a very unique and remarkable facility that we are giving to people of Indian descent who are now citizens of another country. We have also initiated other programs such as the Know India Program, know India Quiz and the like for the youth. We also provide about 240 scholarship. Through these efforts, we are seeking to connect and collaborate, in an effort to contribute to each other welfare.

# NEIGHBOURS AND THE NEIGHBOURHOOD

# 17

# India's Neighbourhood: An Evolving Concept

*Amar Sinha*

How do we define India's neighbourhood? Does it refer to our immediate neighbourhood, determined by geography; is it shaped by history or is it shaped by political impulses that are beyond our control? Do we not consider Indonesia and Cambodia as our neighbours based on our ancient links? What about the neighbours across the seas? Answering these questions is important to not only understand India's core national interests but also in determining an optimum foreign policy for India. In British India, our neighbours were different. The partition shrunk our borders and creation of Pakistan and its illegal occupation of parts of Jammu and Kashmir made us lose our borders with Iran and Afghanistan, as also access and connectivity with Central Asia. Over time borders do change and new neighbours arise either through expansion, such as China's expansion into and annexation of Tibet, or the birth of a new nation, such as Bangladesh. Therefore, it is clear that the concept of 'neighbourhood' is not a static one.

Each such impediment, however, also leads to innovation. When we lost direct connectivity to Afghanistan it prompted the search for alternative routes. As a result India is now connected to Afghanistan via Iran and its Chabahar port. I would also like to point out that as a nation we are more aware of our neighbours on the West, and most only have a fuzzy idea of our neighbours on the East. There is also a greater awareness of our land neighbours while we tend to forget our maritime neighbours such as Thailand, Indonesia, Oman or even East Africa. Perhaps this is the result of the threats that emanated from the West. This also leads us to the concept of 'extended neighbourhood' which is often used while formulating India's foreign policy.

In ancient India, our culture, religion and empires spread right from Indonesia to Cambodia, all of which formed a part of our zone of influence. In a way the British aided in extending our people connect and 'neighbourhood' by taking people to far off places as Mauritius and Fiji among other countries further away. Today, we are rightly looking at the Indo-Pacific as our extended neighbourhood. Therefore, nations can define neighbourhood depending on their national interests, core security and strategic concerns and areas to which, as a nation, they feel connected to. All these factors determine our neighbourhood policy. Thus, I would aver that the Gulf or East Africa is as much our neighbour as nations in the SAARC region.

In the ASEAN context we have the three C's—culture, connectivity and commerce—that drive our foreign policy initiatives. Similarly, the concept of the five S's—Samriddhi, Suraksha, Samman, Samvad and Sanskriti—have gained salience in our immediate neighbourhood, particularly as the current South Asia is only a fragmented India of the past.

The creation of SAARC in 1985 was to boost the three C's and the five S's. We need to remember that connectivity, both people to people connectivity and physical connectivity is a lynchpin in our South Asian policy. In fact, when we look at SAARC, it becomes clear that only India shares common borders with other SAARC countries, (expect for Pakistan sharing a border with Afghanistan), giving India a central role in initiating connectivity policies.

Given the size of India within South Asia, many analysts make the mistake of describing India as a big brother, overlooking the ground reality. In fact India in a benevolent power that is a key to the South Asian identity and mutual connectivity. Accordingly, most of our policies have been non-reciprocal, which is not based on a quid pro quo. For example, to benefit all our neighbours from the growing and large Indian market, we created a special window for the least developed countries (LDCs) within SAARC and granted a zero duty access to India for all their products. However, since SAARC itself became moribund, we had to evolve a mechanism for SAARC-minus one with a special focus on sub-regional cooperation. This led to the formations of BIMSTEC. Our size and centrality is thus a key determinant of our neighbourhood policy, driven by the motto enunciated by Prime Minister Modi—'Sabka Saath, Sabka Vikas'.

Accordingly, after May 2014, our outreach to the neighbourhood has intensified and added new dimensions to the earlier objectives of connectivity. This new dimension relates to security. It hardly needs emphasis that for continued and rapid economic growth, security is essential. India is also aware that as it rises economically, it will necessarily have to carry its neighbours together with it and this would entail greater regional integration and providing greater access to Indian markets and opportunities arising from its growth. We have to build a consensus on this idea of shared destiny and shared prosperity in our region. This is a key to our successful neighbourhood policy.

Another element of India's regional policies is how we interact with the political forces in the region. Evidently a policy where India starts picking the winners and losers will not be sustainable, so our efforts have to be directed at building excellent relations with all nations and entire spectrum of political forces therein, but even more importantly, deepening our mutual trust through closer people-to-people connect.

A major factor that will guide our policy is the fact that India has become a net provider of security and humanitarian assistance in the region. Since we don't have expansionist designs it becomes easy for us. The Doklam incident is a clear cut case where India came in support of a small neighbour, or in an emergency in Nepal, where, in the wake of a massive earthquake, India was the first responder. We have also undertaken such HADR actions in Maldives and Yemen to name a few. This is a reflection of our growing capabilities and a changed India.

Domestically, we will have to increasingly include and work with our states that share common borders with our regional neighbours. If they are part of the decision making process, they become stakeholders and we will be better able to manage the challenges that we face such as illegal immigration, smuggling and drug trafficking. The trend globally too is states and regions becoming active participants in foreign policy formulation. I love to cite the case of the Ganga Water treaty with Bangladesh in 1996 when both the Government in West Bengal and Delhi cooperated, a long festering issue got resolved. Similarly, the recent Land Boundary Agreement (LBA) with Bangladesh is also an excellent example of Centre and State collaborating to resolve legacy issues. Another example is the cooperation of Bihar government in providing electricity transmission lines to Nepal and Nepal's cooperation with India to mitigate the floods affecting Bihar.

One key advantage that India has, is in terms of enhancing skills all around. India has become a hub for education and is attracting people for short-term courses, like languages, computers training, accountancy and auditing and IT networking. Protection of our diaspora and providing HADR assistance has also emerged as a very important aspect of our policy and we have seen its positive impact on regional trust building and cooperation.

Finally, to all students of public policy making, I can give only one advice based on my personal experience and that is to believe that India has a message and it is heard around the world, and more so in our immediate vicinity. So, it is required that we articulate our positions clearly and share our views with our friends in clear terms. Also we should take a common and tough stand against rogue nations. In the past, India's message was couched in too many layers of diplomatic language that left people puzzled as to what exactly did India want. We never asked for what we wanted clearly. This has changed now and as a practitioner I can say with confidence that our messaging and our expectations are both quite clear. Finally, Samriddhi (prosperity), Suraksha (security), Samman (respect), Samvad (dialogue) and Sanskriti (culture) should remain the bedrock of our foreign policy.

# 18

## Neighbourhood Policies

*Sanjaya Baru*

In the two books that I have written, my stance on international relations and foreign policy is that it stands on the base of economic policies. Unless you are clear on your economic aspirations one cannot formulate foreign policy. It is not culture, nor politics, nor security. These three are all important, but the modern world's stand on this is that a nation's foreign policy is defined by economic interest. So, when discussing the neighbourhood, let me go back to economics.

There is a difference between neighbours and neighbourhood and in international relation, neighbourhood is decided by community. Neighbours are given by geography, like who lives above your flat. But neighbourhood is bonded via relations and initiative, much akin to people living together in a colony and coming together for group activities, and becoming a common part of that endeavour.

But the biggest confusion in India's foreign policy has been the confusion between these two. In 2012, on a day when the then Prime Minister Manmohan Singh was meeting ASEAN leaders, the ministry had launched a website. Right on top of the website, SAARC was mentioned as neighbourhood. I called the Minister and told him of the contradiction. The Prime Minister was meeting ASEAN leaders to develop the neighbourhood, whereas the website gave an idea that the neighbourhood was already developed. This contradiction was not individual but conceptual.

In 1945, KM Pannikar, in his book *India and the Indian Ocean: An Essay on the Influence of Sea Power on Indian History*, drew attention to the fact that

British empire had created a steel ring for the defence of India, with fortified bases at Socotra, Mauritius and Singapore.[1] Recently, in January 2018, India's Foreign Secretary, S. Jaishankar and Secretary of State of Seychelles, Ambassador Barry Faure signed an agreement for the development, management, operation and maintenance of facilities on Assumption Island. This was a sequel to Prime Minister Narendra Modi's visit to Seychelles in 2015, where both countries had inked an agreement to develop infrastructure on Assumption Island. Seychelles lies just below Socotra, so we are now finally reestablishing our presence there and are also reviving our relations with Socotra, Mauritius and Singapore. Pannikar had brought attention to this because he said India's borders are not just geographical borders like the Himalayas and the oceans.

In another fascinating book *Caravans: Indian Merchants on the Silk Road*, Scott C. Levi tells the fascinating story of tens of thousands of intrepid Multani and Shikarpuri merchants, who travelled great distances across Afghanistan, Iran, Central Asia and on to St Petersburg in Russia. As we celebrate the relations with ASEAN countries, who have similar cultures, temples, etc., these are our true neighbourhood. Why did we allow all this to vanish? The partition of India was one of the causative factors, but a major reason was also the fact that post-1947, India turned inwards and became insular. Trade declined and there was huge reduction in foreign investments and exports, based on the assumption that India was self-sufficient and could produce enough for itself. For 30 years we destroyed our relations with the world. And it was only in 1991, that India re-opened her gates. But the damage was done. India's long-standing relations with the Arab world was ruined. It must be remembered that the Rupee was a negotiable currency in the Arab world and also in Singapore. I was told by a friend in Bahrain that his grandfather travelled to Mecca via Bombay, because the only link from Bahrain was the sea link. So one took a boat to Mumbai and thence to Aden and Mecca, which simply showed how the Arab was culturally and economically integrated with India. So was Southeast Asia.

Why was Southeast Asia referred to as Indo-China by the Europeans? It was because the mass of land, bound by the Indian Subcontinent in the west and China in the north, and corresponding to the present-day areas of Cambodia, Thailand, Laos, Myanmar, Vietnam, and (variably) peninsular Malaysia and Singapore, were lands historically within the cultural influence of India and China, and Europeans found strong Indian presence here. But we ruined all that by turning inwards. Now, we have started getting that relationship back, and we are integrating. The problem for India is that China started the reintegration process much earlier and India now has to compete with Chinese dominance. Even in SAARC, China has become the biggest trading partner. We do not do enough trade with our neighbours, except perhaps with Bhutan. Sans the economic angle, other nations would have precious little to do with India as it would yield no economic advantage. This is the base of the Arthashastra. And we can increase our economic base and those of our neighbours by spreading our horizons and increasing our trading base.

There seems to be a change in approach now, but the simple movement of people between countries will not force change. We need to look into movement of goods and services. India's neighbourhood policy can be revived by creating and reviving interdependent economic relations that we already had, but lost. We need to strike right relations with right deals.

## NOTE

[1]Panikkar, KM, *India And the Indian Ocean: An essay on the influence of sea power on Indian History*, George Allen and Unwin, London, 1945.

# 19

# The Af-Pak Region: Why Turmoil Will Remain

*Vivek Katju*

India's current relations with Pakistan and Afghanistan can best be understood in the context of certain historical truths. This region to the west of India, was historically, for very long periods, a part of India. For instance, over 2300 years ago, the boundaries of the Mauryan Empire stretched up to and beyond the Hindu Kush Mountain ranges. In the middle ages, the Mughals too, for a long period had a large part of what is present-day Afghanistan under their rule. And in the British era, what is now Pakistan and India were one unit. An understanding of India's relations with its western neighbours hence cannot be divorced from the historical context.

The first question that comes to mind is, why did Pakistan come into being? This is significant and important to focus on, because to a very large extent, the problems that bedevil India-Pakistan relations lie rooted in that history. Partition of India was a consequence of the two-nation theory propounded by Mohd Ali Jinnah, the founder of Pakistan who headed the Muslim League for a long time. It was the Muslim League that propagated the division of the country on religious lines, and the carving out of a separate homeland for the Muslims. Jinnah and the Muslim League believed that religion constitutes the basic ingredient of a nation, and therefore Hindus and Muslims who lived in India, comprised not just two separate nations but two separate antagonistic nations that could never live together. This was expounded by Jinnah is his address in Lahore in 1940. "it is extremely difficult" Jinnah said, "to appreciate why our Hindu friends fail to understand the real nature of Islam and Hinduism. They are not religions in the strict sense of the word, but are, in fact, different and distinct social orders; and it is a dream that the Hindus and Muslims can ever evolve a common nationality; and this misconception of one Indian nation has gone far beyond the limits and is the cause of more of our troubles and will lead India to destruction if we fail to revise our notions in time. The Hindus and Muslims belong to two different religious philosophies, social customs, and literature. They neither intermarry nor inter-dine together, and indeed they belong to two different civilisations which are based mainly on conflicting ideas and conceptions. Their aspects on life, and of life, are different. It is quite clear that Hindus and Mussalmans derive their inspiration from different sources of history. They have different epics, their heroes are different, and different episode. Very often the hero of one is a foe of the other, and likewise their victories and defeats overlap. To yoke together two such nations under a single state, one as a numerical minority and the other as a majority, must lead to growing discontent, and final destruction of any fabric that may be so built up for the government of such a state."[1] While Jinnah was not the first to propound the two-nation theory, he gave the concept political legitimacy, which led to the creation of Pakistan as a separate homeland for the Muslims.

The real basis for the formation of Pakistan was thus Jinnah's and the Muslim Leagues' view that Hindus and Muslims are two separate nations. The Congress Party, which led India's Freedom Movement, and other parties too, opposed this view holding that while religion is important in life, it cannot be the basis for the formation of a state. However, India was partitioned on religious lines. While Pakistan became an Islamic State, India chose secularism and an inclusive democracy. But Pakistan, having internalised the Muslim League view that Hindus and Muslims could not live together, remains antagonistic to India and believes India to be a perpetual enemy and a threat to its very existence. Pakistan is, what India is not. It is in essence, the very antithesis of what India stands for. This remains the basic problem, from which flows the chill in India-Pakistan relations and makes the management of India-Pakistan relations such a difficult proposition. This idea of Muslim nationhood remains the cause of the Kashmir problem. The state of Jammu and Kashmir (J&K) acceded to India, despite having a majority Muslim population, and this was anathema to Pakistan, which was formed on the basis of religious identity.

Over the last 70 years, successive Indian governments have tried to inject an element of positivity into the India-Pakistan relationship by trying to convince the Pakistani establishment that India poses no threat to that state, but desires friendship and cooperation. Mr Vajpayee, as Prime Minister, undertook a very significant visit to Lahore by bus in 1999. He even visited the Minar-e-Pakistan in Lahore, a monument erected at the place where the Muslim League adopted the Pakistan Resolution, well knowing that many people in India would not like that gesture and wrote in the visitors book that a stable and secure Pakistan is in India's interest. But he did that to convey to the people of Pakistan that partition was a fact of history and that India had no interest in undoing Pakistan. The present government too has tried to build relationships with Pakistan, and the manifestation of that has been Prime Minister Modi going out of his way to build friendship, but all attempts to do so have floundered because of the negative responses that keep emanating from Pakistan.

During the last three decades or more, especially from 1990 onwards, Pakistan has also perfected the art of intervening in the internal processes of India, using agitation and terrorism as an instrument of state policy. Despite that, India continued to make efforts to reach out to Pakistan with a view to resolving differences peacefully. Towards that end, in December 2015 a dialogue structure was to begin. The External Affairs Minister, Shrimati Sushma Swaraj went to Islamabad and on the margins of an international conference that dialogue structure was determined. Prime Minister Modi then undertook a diplomatically spectacular visit to Pakistan, stopping over at Lahore while returning to New Delhi from Kabul, where he interacted with the Pakistani premier. But that process too was sabotaged by the Pakistan Army, by a series of provocative terrorist attacks against India. So, India-Pakistan relations remain strained, primarily because of the Pakistani mindset that India is an existential threat to Pakistan.

With respect to Afghanistan, the interests of both India and Afghanistan are aligned, with India wanting a bilateral relationship with Afghanistan in line with what the Afghans want. But this is anathema to Pakistan, which wants a virtual veto on Afghanistan's India policy and that is something that no Afghan government is willing to accommodate. Both Afghanistan's erstwhile President Mr Karzai and the present incumbent, Mr Ghani have repeatedly reached out to Pakistan with the message that Afghanistan wants a balanced relationship in the region and that they will not choose between India and Pakistan. However, this has found little traction in the Pakistani establishment, especially with its Army, which seeks to play a dominant role in Afghanistan's affair through the Afghan Taliban, which the Pakistan military nurtures and supports, in its attempts to intervene in domestic processes of Afghanistan. The Afghan Taliban operates from sanctuaries and safe havens in Pakistan and is sponsored by the Pakistani establishment to create mayhem in Afghanistan. India has not interfered in the Afghanistan–Pakistan relationship, as it considers the matter a bilateral issue and has never sought to use Afghan territory to influence Pakistan. But Pakistan is wary of the India–Afghanistan relationship, because it fears that India can encircle Pakistan from the East as well as from the West.

It is the Indian vision that Afghanistan should be a link country, which enables the flow of trade, energy and people from Central Asia to South Asia—the great Asian roundabout, as said by the Afghan President, leading to harmony and prosperity within Afghanistan and in the surrounding region. But Pakistan's desire to control Kabul's India policy has ensured that this idea does not fructify. So the picture is pessimistic, primarily because of the fundamental reflexes of the Pakistani establishment towards the region—reflexes that are militaristic and believe in force and terror as instruments of state policy. The Afghan Taliban is Pakistan's instrument in Afghanistan. The Lashkar-e-Taiba, Jaish-e-Mohammed and such like terrorist organisations are Pakistan's instruments to be used against India.

The international community is aware of the destabilising role being played by Pakistan, and has conveyed its concerns to Pakistan that this must end. But, unfortunately, as long as effective pressure on the ground is not brought to bear on Pakistan it has simply no incentive to change. As of now, President Trump too has ratcheted up pressure against Pakistan, but in essence his approach is no different from those of his predecessors. The present state is hence likely to continue.

## NOTE

[1]Presidential address by Muhammad Ali Jinnah to the Muslim League, Lahore, 1940, available at http://www.columbia.edu/itc/mealac/pritchett/00islamlinks/txt_jinnah_lahore_1940.html

# 20

## The Af–Pak Region: A Role for India

*Amar Sinha*

Foreign policy issues with respect to both Afghanistan and Pakistan are perhaps the most widely covered in the Indian media. Everybody has an opinion on Pakistan and on how India should deal with that country. It is a fact that in Afghanistan, the fund of goodwill that India has, is perhaps unmatched by any other country. But the public perception that India is the largest donor to Afghanistan is not factual. India's total commitments to Afghanistan are huge, but many countries have made larger commitments. For example, Sweden spends per annum in Afghanistan, more than what India invests. India's investments are in large projects and so can vary from year to year. But India is committed to the development of Afghanistan and has stayed the course. India has never spoken of an exit policy and this fact is very reassuring to the people of Afghanistan.

There has been a spurt in the intensity of violence in Afghanistan since May 2017. In January 2018, there was an attack on the Intercontinental Hotel in Kabul in which 22 people were killed. In retaliation, US drones killed three Haqqani leaders in FATA. Violence continues unabated, which has led to pessimism and a feeling that the situation is unlikely to improve. Every year, 8000 Afghan soldiers are killed in the ongoing conflict. The civilians too suffer, with 5000 civilians getting killed or injured each year. Such heavy losses are unsustainable, but on the positive side, the Afghan Army has no shortage of recruits, which helps to maintain the strength of the army at present levels. Another matter of concern is the high levels of desertions that take place in the Afghan Army, but these are seasonal desertions for agriculture. Afghans have tremendous resilience and have great love for their country, and while desertions are a matter of concern, it is unlikely that the deserters will join the Afghan Taliban.

The US intervention in Afghanistan in 2001 remains the longest war that the US has fought. But it must be remembered that Afghanistan was peaceful for five years till 2005. People could take taxis from Kandahar to Kabul or from Mazar-i-Sharif to Kabul without any fear. This was made possible because the US was incensed with the attack on its territory in September 2001 and Pakistan was aware that if provoked, the Americans would hit them hard. Unfortunately, at this time, the US took their eyes of the ball and got involved in a costly campaign in Iraq. This gave Pakistan the opportunity that they were seeking. They realised that the US may not stay the course and that they simply had to ensure that the Afghan Taliban remained relevant in the emerging scenario. And this allowed the Afghan Taliban to become a force to reckon with, especially as it had secure bases in Pakistan.

President Trump has now come down hard on Pakistan and the US has also de-hyphenated India and Pakistan from its Afghanistan policy. The earlier narrative was mindful of Pakistan's concerns and voices were consistently raised that India is a provocation and must cut down its role in Afghanistan to assuage the Pakistani establishment. The narrative that was sought to be spread was that India's development assistance was not contributing to peace and security in Afghanistan but was a destabilising factor. This false narrative has now been exposed and President Trump is welcoming an increased role for India. This obviously does not imply a military role, which India is wary off. It is more in terms of training the Afghan security forces, facilitating economic development and providing assistance for nation building. India responded, and her commitment is open ended, as repeatedly reiterated by Prime Minister Narendra Modi. President Trump has also stated that he will walk the talk and if required take recourse to conflict to force the Afghan Taliban to the negotiating table. This has been a clear message to the Taliban and its supporters, but we still have to see how this will pan out. Hopefully, it will lead to change.

China continues to use the Pakistani talking points and projects the Pakistani perspective. In the process, China tries to assuage the Afghan government by saying that Pakistan needs more time, and is making efforts for peace, but the argument is not convincing. A matter of concern is the new divergence that is coming about, where countries like Russia and Iran are veering around to the view that the root cause of the problem or the major source of concern in Afghanistan comes from the Islamic State Khorasan (IS-K)[1] rather than from the Afghan Taliban. This is an interesting development. Of the two major attacks which took place recently, the first one, which was a bomb blast near the old Indian embassy was claimed by the Taliban. The next attack, a day later, on a military target was immediately claimed by the Islamic State.

A great deal of care needs to be exercised by analysts while assessing the threat in Afghanistan. The intelligence agencies as well as public perception in Afghanistan is very clear that there is no Islamic State presence in Afghanistan, at least not the way its presence is felt in Syria. What seems to be unfolding is a new avatar of the game that Pakistan has been playing in the region, because its links with the Afghan Taliban has been exposed. The new Pakistani narrative is seeking to distance the Afghan Taliban from the violence in Afghanistan and put the onus of creating instability in Afghanistan on the Islamic State. This gives Pakistan an element of deniability, enabling it to pin the violence in Afghanistan on the Islamic State and opening up the possibility of the Taliban coming back to power in Afghanistan in some form. This narrative needs to be countered and not allowed to spread. Unfortunately, the Russians have bought into this, because they want to tell the US that their policies in Afghanistan have failed. The failure of the USSR in Afghanistan still rankles the Russians.

Iran too is known to be hedging its bets with some elements of Taliban, which will create fissures within the Taliban. The senseless attack near the Indian embassy was actually criticised by the Mullah Rasool led Taliban faction. Mullah Rasool leads an important military faction of Taliban and he was one of the front runners to replace Mullah Omar. His criticism of the attack, as also the wide abhorrence expressed by the Afghan people on the same shows that perhaps the tide is turning in some manner and that senseless violence can only lead to the Taliban getting marginalised and losing public support. As of now, the Taliban hopes to get back to power, but it would be very difficult for any government to co-opt them into any power sharing arrangement, if they continue with this policy.

In such a scenario, what are the likely Indian options? It is important for India to keep exposing the duality in Pakistan's policy and to reject the insidious linkage that Pakistan wants to create that what they are doing in Afghanistan is basically because there is a threat from India. This is blatantly false as there is nothing that India is doing in Afghanistan which is not done in consultation with the Afghan government and with full transparency.

Pakistan claims that India has 24 consulates all over Afghanistan. This charge is absurd. On being questioned about this claim, the Pakistani embassy maintained a studied silence. Second, the Pakistanis have been accusing India of using Kandahar and Helmand to destabilise Baluchistan. This charge too is preposterous. Both Kandahar and Helmand have seen the largest presence of American and British soldiers for the last 15 years. It would not be possible for any country to carry out such activities without the coalition forces getting to know of it. India does not need a land route to enter Baluchistan. Just as the Pakistani terrorists reached Mumbai by boat in November 2008, it is possible to reach Baluchistan by sea, considering the huge coastline that Baluchistan has. But the fact is it is not Indian policy to create trouble in Pakistan. If credence is to be given to such a Pakistani narrative, then it would seem that Pakistan has a much bigger problem on its hands, for it would mean that both the US and UK are turning a blind eye to Indian actions!

India of course will continue to support the government and people of Afghanistan, who look up to India as a major voice for them and for their government. Their diplomatic reach is still limited so they feel that India is a big voice to articulate their side of the story, and seek its support. They expect India to remain open to them for trade and commerce because even today, despite the difficulties, 40 per cent of Afghanistan's total global exports are to India. This used to be 100 per cent prior to independence and even post-independence when there were no barriers placed on trade by Pakistan. So Afghanistan has a huge dependency on India in terms of trade, and rightly so as India is a very large market close to it. It also seeks India's support in education, health, trade, commerce and economic development.

One thing that continues to baffle Pakistan is Afghanistan's friendship with India as they keep harping on the differences in religion. They question why Afghanistan, a Muslim state is friends with a Hindu majority India? Pakistan views relationships in binaries, which is not the case with Afghanistan. Historically, Afghanistan has had a close connect with India for different reasons and this still resonates and is remembered in Afghanistan.

The world needs to understand that what is happening to Pakistan is a blowback of the policy followed by its military and generals who have promoted terrorism, using it as an instrument of state policy. The articulation and execution of a policy of bleeding India with a thousand cuts, which Pakistan is also applying to Afghanistan, has consequences, the most important being that the terror organisations so created invariably bite the hand that feeds it. Unless Pakistan reverses these policies, peace will be an unlikely outcome in the region. It will also lead to increased violence levels within Pakistan which will bring down the Pakistani state.

## NOTE

[1]The Islamic State announced its expansion to the Khorasan region in 2015, which historically encompasses parts of modern day Iran, Central Asia, Afghanistan, and Pakistan.

# 21

## India–China Relations

*Ashok Kantha*

There was a report in the Facebook entry of a District Magistrate in Uttar Pradesh, which was subsequently withdrawn. It said that why were hooligans shouting anti-Pakistan slogans when they should have been shouting anti-China slogans as China is the bigger enemy. This reflects a particular stereotype, a binary perception of China which is becoming more and more prevalent. Increasingly, we are looking at China in terms of not friends but as an adversary or threat. I will offer a slightly different perspective, a perspective of someone who was engaged in dealing with China in the Ministry of External Affairs for over 30 years, and that is that we must acknowledge the complexities of this relationship with respect to many issues and avoid a binary approach when dealing with China.

Contrary to popular perception, our China policy has been successful in recent years. We have developed a pragmatic approach, one of recognising outstanding issues and trying to deal with them, while at the same time, trying not to let those differences define our engagement. The focus has been on compartmentalising the problems and not letting differences turn into disputes. A particular understanding has been arrived at by Prime Minister Narendra Modi and President Xi Jinping in 2017 and we are looking to continuously explore areas of convergence and cooperation in multilateral domains. This approach has served both sides well. It is different from Pakistan where we get bogged down by differences and windows of possibilities are often found to be shut. But that is not the experience I had with China, where our report card has been relatively impressive. For one, the leaders of both countries have invested in this relationship as seen by the number of Summit meetings which have taken place. The borders between the two countries are peaceful in spite of problems in perception of the boundary and Line of Actual Control. We have differences, but all these can be discussed.

Today, India and China are engaged more than ever before. There is substantial economic relation and an increasing people-to-people contact. There are more than 18,000 Indian students studying in China and the Indian film, 'Dangal,' was a massive hit in China. There is substantial cooperation between the two countries in working together on regional, multilateral and global issues. But, despite these positive elements, we are today at an inflexion point in our relationship. We need a new beginning, a new paradigm which means that something in the old is not in order. Relations have entered a more challenging phase and remain a mix of cooperation and complication.

How is India going to pursue its relationship with an increasingly assertive China, in an international context which is uncertain? Let us first look into some of the challenges and the roots of certain anxieties in the India-China relationship. Today, India-China relations are surfing in the overhang of issues pertaining to security and defence. A great deal has appeared in the media about Chinese support to Pakistan on the issue of Masood Azhar, the Doklam standoff between India and China and Chinese stand on the NSG waiver to India. These are not new issues, but their articulation in the public domain has led to a negative cycle of action-reaction which has coloured the perception about India-China relations. A second set of challenges arise due to the fact that bilateral difference acquired greater prominence because of geopolitical issues. India and China have different perspectives in Asia-Pacific region and globally. There are growing regional concerns in India about China's regional and global ambitions. This pattern has been self-evident. For instance, at the 19th Congress, Xi Jinping in his work report came out very clearly with an explicit agenda on China in terms of its role. He said bluntly that China will realign itself at the top of the world by 2050. We are witnessing a more assertive China in its international behaviour, which is reflected in so many different areas such as willingness to deploy military strength to achieve its strategic objectives and trying to seize the present conducive environment which is assessed by Chinese as a period of strategic opportunity, especially when USA under Trump is perceived to be in retreat.

China is trying to seek equal status with US as a superpower and reemergence in Asia-Pacific, but eventually, it wants global leadership. This also came out in the US National Strategic Defense Paper of 19 January 2018, which stated that China seeks Indo-Pacific hegemony in the near term and displacement of US to seek global pre-eminence in the future. I am inclined to agree with this assessment. China is no longer interested in a multipolar world, which is where its position diverges from India's. India would not only like to see a multipolar world but a multipolar Asia, whereas Chinese preference increasingly is for a hierarchical order where it moves towards the top. There are concerns from the Chinese side too, with respect to India's growing alignment with USA, Japan and others which is seen as a bid to constrain China.

A third set of concerns today arise from the fact that there is growing complication, in both land and maritime arena. China is seen to be increasingly less sensitive to India's interests as seen by its proximity to Pakistan, where it has invested heavily in the strategic domain as also in the China-Pakistan Economic Corridor (CPEC). Its development of the Gwadar port could potentially emerge as a naval facility for China on the lines of the Djibouti port which provides facilities to the US, French and Chinese navies. China's expanding footprint in Indian Ocean Region and the emerging contestation in Indian Ocean is also a source of concern. China's One Belt One Road (OBOR) initiative is seen by China as an economic issue, but India has many reservations, not least of which is that the CPEC, an important constituent of the OBOR, passes through Indian territory in Pakistan Occupied J&K. It is also seen as changing India's operational environment.

The fourth set of concerns arises out of the boundary question which had receded, but is now centre stage, after the Doklam face-off. It represents a trend in the way China defines its core interests including contested territorial claims. In the South China Sea, China took a position that its core interests are non-negotiable and it will not make any concessions though they are contested territorial claims and other countries have a very different view and a very different position. India's challenge will be in managing anxieties arising out of an assertive China with the scenario of an increasing capability gap between the two countries. At present, the Chinese GDP is five times the size of India's GDP and its defence budget is four and one half times more than India's defence budget. This is a huge gap and is unlikely to be made up in the near future.

A nuanced approach is suggested to manage elements of cooperation and competition. It will be desirable to keep relations on an even level and seek constructive growth trajectories despite challenges. Any across the border intervention against China will be counterproductive as it will distract India from her primary national endeavour of nation building. Perhaps, we will like to take a leaf out of China's book of dealing with USA, where till recently, it preferred to bide its time and focussed on building its own capacity rather than taking on the USA head on. Simultaneously, it is important that we invest in developing deterrence vis-a-vis China. Deterrence will be through asymmetric response, not just by developing defensive capabilities but by developing offensive capabilities as well, particularly in the maritime domain. India needs a balancing partnership with the USA, Japan, Vietnam and others given the capability gap that it has with China. At the same time, it will be important for India to ensure that it is not saddled with a junior partner's role in the Indo-Pacific region. A closer strategic dialogue is required to manage these relations and to build new relationships and an important aspect will be to build on the understandings which have already been made.

India and China need to engage with each other and look into leveraging opportunities that come out of this engagement. Even though there are many challenges in the relationship, China is the second largest economy in the world and presents India with huge opportunities as an important source of FDI in India, particularly in the services sector where our engagement is expanding. But we are far from a satisfactory position. We are nowhere in the picture when it comes to production supply chains laid to China, which has become a major driver in global economic growth. A second example would relate to Modi's visit to China in May 2015, which recognised the fact that simultaneous reemergence of India and China as two major powers and how to deal with it, is going to be a primary challenge. The development of such a template must perforce be mindful of each other's concerns and aspirations. How to translate the template in specific issues in terms of challenges requires closer dialogue, accommodating each other. It calls for better communication between the two countries. Looking beyond bilateral relations, there is a need to forge a fresh agenda for collaboration in multilateral and global issues. Both countries have made progress but India does have a divergent strategic perspective and forging a fresh agenda will not be easy.

The good news for both India and China is that despite their differences, huge opportunities exist for mutual benefit. Both sides recognise the importance of keeping relations in constructive trajectories despite numerous challenges. That is a good basis on which to try and develop this relationship and avoid a path of confrontation, which will not be in the interest of either country.

# 22

# Contestation in the India-China Context

*Harsh V Pant*

As a student of international relations I would try to conceptualise the elements of the India-China relationship. A good starting point would be to think about the 2017 Doklam standoff, for it is emblematic of the current India-China relations. Those who follow Indian foreign policy and Sino-Indian relations closely were taken aback by the incident, because this was something that no one had predicted would happen and which even our diplomats did not think was hovering on the Sino-Indian landscape. So I think at some level we were not prepared for what was happening on the border. The confidence that some of us had in the ability of this relationship to manage the border was perhaps a bit misplaced, especially the argument that the border with Pakistan is very volatile, but we have managed our borders with China very well and that is certainly a tribute to good diplomacy.

However, the underlying realities were such that something like Doklam was bound to happen one way or another. And when the standoff between the two countries took place, it lasted all of 73 days, before both the parties went back to their original positions—the move coming significantly days before the BRICS summit was scheduled to be held in China from 3-5 September 2017. Only after the announcement of disengagement by both sides did the path for the 2017 edition of the BRICS summit got cleared. Thereafter, when the leaders of the two countries, Prime Minister Narendra Modi of India and President Xi Jinping of China met at the Summit, it underlined the ability of the two countries to manage disputes, if not to resolve them. But the reality also remains, that the underlying forces that are pushing this relationship in a certain direction remain where they were pre-Doklam.

Let us take a look at the structural realities. The structure of the international environment is in flux and is uncertain. The traditional power structures are disappearing, certain powers are rising and some powers are falling. The certainty and the certitude with which we have lived since the end of the Cold War is disappearing in front of our eyes and the idea that new power realities and new power configurations are emerging is now taken as a given. Those who have read Paul Kennedy's book, *The Rise and Fall of Great Powers*, well know that when great powers rise, they rise at the expense of others and that has an impact on the neighbourhood, on the international system and on the international order.

As China rises, it is but natural that it will try to expand its footprint. It is also very natural that this will cause a lot of consternation in its neighbourhood, especially in those areas where countries are most vulnerable. So you see sudden problems in its vicinity, such as in the South China Sea and the widening of territorial disputes in South Asia. It is also intruding into India's sphere of influence. This is a structural reality that India is confronting and it is compounded by the fact that India too is rising. And India too is responding to its own economic, military and political might. So we have two powers rising and where China wants a unipolar Asia, India wants a multipolar Asia, leading naturally to contestation.

Post the Cold War, when the United States was the sole super power, Russia, China and India in trilateral fora would bemoan American uni-polarity. They still do so and seek a multi-polar world, but with China's rise, its idea of a multipolar world order looks very different from the Indian or even the Russian idea. These contestations are inevitable and we will have very different understandings of what kind of geospatial matrix is going to emerge from our perspective and from the perspective of other nations.

In a sense, the unique situation arising out of a unipolar world order helped both India and China to develop to integrate globally and to reap the benefits of globalisation. It is now time to confront the reality of the emergence in due course of a bipolar or multipolar world order. After arguing for multipolarity for so long, we are now confronted with the consequences of what happens when a multipolar world order emerges and one that is not going to be seamless. There will be multiple alignments, multiple coalitions, multiple partnerships that countries have to engage with and that again is being reflected in the way countries, especially India, are trying to manage their relationships. That is why India has invested in BRICS and is trying to do something with the Quad—the US, Japan, India and Australia initiative in the Indo-Pacific. This then is the reality of the world we live in because of the structural changes that are taking place all around us.

China's rise in Asia has a second set of consequences, which is that it is challenging the institutional frameworks and the normative order. So our problem in many ways is that the order through which we have benefited and through which we have lived over the past few decades is also under tremendous stress. When India talks of the Indian Ocean or the South China Sea and it talks with maritime states in the region, it is exactly this point that it is trying to make. When we talk of a free and fair trading system and free sea lanes of communication we are looking at a landscape that is changing and a rising China is challenging some of those normative assumptions which we have held dear for so long. This is the challenge that most countries, including India, are facing, because we see a perceived American retreat and China's rise, both happening at the same time. This means that our ability to manage this change in the normative flux is limited and getting restricted by the day.

There are consequences of this change. In the Indian Ocean and in the South China Sea, it is the maritime order that is the cause of the greatest concern. In Southeast Asia, ASEAN is under tremendous stress, again partly because of what is happening at the structural level. China's ability to divide and rule in the ASEAN is a manifestation of the fact that the ASEAN is now driven from this dissent from within. This is again a reflection of the fact that the certainty of those days when America used to be the security guarantor for Southeast Asia is gone and China's rise is putting tremendous strain on an organisation that was actually built partly to balance China. So we are looking at the consequences of a power transition in the system and these consequences are being felt normatively and institutionally and this is a reflection again of the challenges that states like India continue to confront. We are seeing China's ability to intrude into South Asia and this has consequences for India, which again is a reflection of China's growing economic might. And as China would like to make sure that other states are prevented from emerging, contestation is very natural.

It is therefore no cause for surprise that China does not want India in the Nuclear Suppliers Group, nor is it a surprise that China and Pakistan share a very warm relationship. This also explains why China supports a known terrorist like Masood Azhar, despite China too facing a threat from Islamist extremism. In the Chinese perceptions, anything that thwarts the rise of India will prevent contestation in Asia and when viewed in that light, a lot of what is happening can be explained. This is the prism that enables an understanding of Sino-Indian relations and the sort of contestation that are happening at multiple levels in the region and across the world.

It's also interesting to look at the domestic politics and the economic factors that drive both India and China and also the domestic constituencies in these two countries. Do we have enough domestic stakeholders, for example, in India vested in Sino-Indian relations? It's very interesting that there was a time when books were being written about Chindia, where ministers and government servants would talk of joint India-China collaboration, for example in going out and bidding jointly for oil fields. These constituencies are fast disappearing in India. Even Indian Communist Party members no longer stand up to defend China in public platforms. This is getting increasingly difficult to do because of Chinese actions in the region. The pro-China constituencies in India are disappearing because the larger reality of the India-China relationship has taken over. We need to understand that there are two different political systems and there is often a problem that we do not understand what is happening within China. India does not have enough China experts in the country who actually understand what is happening within China, as a result, the discourse on China tends to be either lopsided or derivative or induced by the happenings in other countries.

But the larger reality is also that between the domestic politics and the domestic societies, the interactions remain relatively limited. India has a problem in understanding the Chinese system, given the authoritarian nature of China and the lack of transparency in the system. As such, we do not know how much China is investing in defence, which has an impact on our own state of defence preparedness. The centralisation of power in China and its huge economic heft is also a matter of concern. China is India's largest trading partner, but the problem is the huge trade deficit in China's favour and how to open up Chinese markets for Indian goods.

As a political scientist, when we view the India-China relationships, we look at constituencies in each country that can promote this relationship at the domestic level. Such constituencies in the India-China context are absent. This perhaps is a reflection of an inability to comprehend the magnitude of the change that is happening in Sino-Indian relations. At the leadership level, President Xi Jinping has articulated a certain approach to world affairs. He has shed the idea that China can stand back and bide its time and firmly believes that China's time has come. He therefore wants to be very assertive in global politics. Similarly, in India, The Narendra Modi led NDA government has a certain view of India's role in the world. Just a few years back, in 2012, India under the Congress-led UPA government was writing documents like Non-alignment 2.0. Today, the Indian Prime Minister is talking of India as a leading power.

There is thus this difference in terms of how we approach the questions from two different perspectives. The new leadership in India has a vision for the country that is distinct from the kind of approach taken earlier about India's role in the world as that of a balancing power—a non-aligned power. That terminology, hopefully has been rightly buried and in its place is a new found assertion of Indian interests and what that means for India. This of course would lead to contestation and would lead to some tussle with countries who don't see eye to eye with India on certain issues. When we do that, an understanding of what is happening in Sino-Indian relations becomes clearer. In that context, the underlying factors, when viewed structurally, through the domestic, political, economic as well as at the individual level, tell a rather pessimistic story.

In the long term, the India-China relationship is going to be a very difficult one to manage and therefore we need the best minds to come together and articulate a policy on how this could be done in the best possible manner, both in the short term as well as in the medium to long term. India's core concern will remain its pursuit of economic upliftment for its people, technological advancement, military modernisation and political advancement, and in this pursuit it would not like to be sidetracked by distractions from China.

# 23

## India and Central Asia

*Rajiv Sikri*

For a better strategic understanding of the region, we need a clearer definition of Central Asia. As I see it, Central Asia includes Middle Asia, and all the territory lying between Russia, China and India. The region has a small population base and is landlocked, but is of strategic significance because of its geographical location as a security space between the bigger powers.

India shares close historical and cultural ties with this part of the world. Consequently, it is through Central Asia that Indian cultural influences travelled to Tibet and China. In the psyche of the Indian people (and vice versa) Central Asia plays an important cultural role. This region lost its importance because the trading routes shifted to the seas from the 16th century onwards. Later, during the Cold War years, these were closed borders. Post-Cold War politics, however, largely centred around Central Asia as the defining feature of the end of the Cold War was the breakup of the Soviet Union. This opened up a new dynamic situation for the region as well as for India.

India's relationship with Central Asia started off with a legacy of friendship and warmth, dating from the Soviet times. There was no conflict of interests, and no legacy of bitterness. This is why, when these countries became independent, they looked to India for development of good and close relations. However, this could not come about because India, while having many connections with Central Asia, did not have physical connectivity, because of the negative attitude of Pakistan. Although Pakistan could not benefit from the situation, neither did India. Therefore, the region's policies were shaped by China and Russia, and the Indian connection with Central Asia became much weaker than the objective circumstances warranted.

Consequently, it has become difficult for India to compete with other countries such as China, Turkey and Russia, especially on the economic front. India has made investments in the region, in particular in the oil and gas sector. Even these sectors faced hurdles since the region looked primarily to the US, which got the majority of the oil and gas contracts. Recently, China has also stepped up its game and sometimes uses underhand methods to obtain contracts. Nevertheless, India has persisted with its presence in the oil and gas sector and we do have some holdings in this region today. It is to India's advantage that Central Asian countries are looking to diversify investments away from China and Russia. Therefore, there is talk of the Turkmenistan-Afghanistan-Pakistan-India Pipeline (TAPI), a new connectivity through the international North-South corridor via Iran and Russia, Chabahar port that could connect India to northern Afghanistan, Iraq and Central Asia. In addition to roads, there are also proposals for railway connectivity too.

It is important to flag here the criticality of Afghanistan to Central Asia. Unless Afghanistan is stable and provides a viable transit route, it is impossible to access Central Asia. Therefore, India's actions in Afghanistan constitute the *sine qua non* to India's Central Asia policy. The second most important country is Iran because, as of today, the only access India has to Central Asia is through Iran, which faces its own problems with US sanctions. As for China, the security threat of China to India from Central Asia arises not so much because China is the dominant power in the region or even Asia, but because it is a neighbour of India. Therefore, what happens in Tibet and Xinjiang is of vital importance to India from a security point of view. This means that India must keep a very close tab on what is happening in Tibet. For China, Tibet is of vital importance. The India-China border is actually an India-Tibet border. This makes Tibet a key factor in India-China relations.

Given this background, how is India developing her relations with Central Asia? There is a clear focus on terrorism and security cooperation. India is a member of the Shanghai Cooperation Organisation (SCO) and is trying to work out a Free Trade Agreement (FTA) with the region. There is progress in IT and pharmaceuticals and there is energy cooperation in oil and gas sectors as well as in accessing the region's uranium reserves. There is better air connectivity today. Central Asia is also used as a route to access Siberia and the Far East.

One factor that we must be alert to is the impact of developments in Central Asia (the Soviet Central Asia) on Xinjiang, as that was the historical border. If the region were to be destabilised in any way, it would be here. This is why the Chinese are so paranoid about Xinjiang, and are constantly trying to expand their sphere of influence in this area to build a buffer zone. However, China cannot entirely insulate itself from what is happening in Soviet Central Asia. At the same time, without Xinjiang there is no contiguity or link between China and Pakistan. Hence, India needs to keep a close watch on developments in Xinjiang.

As for the developments in the Gulf region, it has very close historical linkages to India in terms of both trade and culture. Today, India gets about two-thirds of its oil from the region. More than eight million Indians live here. Both factors contribute to our interdependence. Since this is an area where India has deep interests, elaborate mechanisms have been built for cooperation on defence, security and terrorism. There has been an annual exchange of visits at the summit and ministerial level, which highlights the greater interaction between India and the region. For India, stability in the Gulf is of vital importance. India has to be very active and alert in the region, especially as regional powers like Egypt, Turkey and Saudi Arabia jostle for space to be the leader in the region.

One of the contradictions that we are now witnessing in the region is increased US pressure on Pakistan and Iran. But the US needs Pakistan to get access into Afghanistan. I am not sure how these contradictions will be resolved. As far as India is concerned, this is a very troublesome region, but one that India cannot walk away from due to its proximity to India and also because it is a region where India has many vital interests. Therefore, India's policy has to be to see how to maintain its interests in the region while weaving through the contradictions. As of now, India has maintained a fine balance, and has good relations with Israel, UAE, Saudi Arabia, Oman and Iran.

# 24

# Strengthening the India-ASEAN Relationship

*Jawed Ashraf*

When we speak of Southeast Asia, we must recognise that this is a relatively new geopolitical construct. It is largely the product of colonial times, and particularly from the wartime administrative requirements of British colonial powers. But, for large parts in history, a major part of this region was known as Indo-China. For two and a half millennia, there has been continuous interaction between India and the region; and archeological evidence points to India's presence in the region even in 500 BCE. China has had a long period of influence as have had Islamic and European influences. There have, therefore, been four waves that run through the history of Southeast Asia. There are two important consequences of it for the present time.

One, the region has not only assimilated different faiths, cultures, traditions and practices, but has also developed a strategic approach that taps into its layered history. At the crossroads between two maritime regions, it has also developed an instinct for balancing between major powers competing with each other in the region. It is not uncommon for Southeast Asian countries to simultaneously hedge, balance and bandwagon. The one unifying feature through of all this is that they wish to see the region stable without any collisions between major powers. They will therefore be as alarmed about conflicts between China and the United States as they will be about US retrenchment in the region or domination by one country. This is something that India is very conscious of in our approach to Southeast Asia. We see ourselves as enhancing the balance and stability in the region.

Two, there is a return to history as the colonial past fades away. We see China's dominant rise as we do India's growth and footprint expanding. There is a feeling in the region that the future may see China and India competing. However, there is a third factor—the United States. For the US, the Western Pacific is a security perimeter. There is a much higher level of engagement in Trump's administration with Southeast Asia than there was under the Obama Presidency. This triangulation is shaping politics here. The region is a contested region and the tensions are obvious. What is the role that ASEAN has played? ASEAN as a project has been a great stabiliser in the region and has the potential to be a great influencer. ASEAN has been a combination of two factors. One, is internal consolidation to create unity. Second, it has expanded its external outreach to ASEAN+8 to include Russia and USA. One manifestation of this is the East Asia Summit.

India has been an important factor. India's trade is 2.6 per cent of ASEAN trade, and its investments are 1.3 per cent of total inflows into ASEAN. Yet, there is great importance attached to relations with India and our presence in the region. It is largely a strategic project. This fits in neatly with the evolving concept of the Indo-Pacific. The Indo-Pacific is in many ways not inconsistent with ASEAN unity and centrality; geographically it places ASEAN at the centre and strategically ASEAN is also driving the Indo-Pacific process through RCEP and East Asia Summit, which map onto the geography of Indo Pacific, though they are not yet comfortable with the term.

From India's perspective, Act East is not just a rhetoric. Firstly, all of India's emerging major partners lie to India's east, including North America. Secondly, what happens in the South China Sea and the Pacific and the Straits of Malacca have a profound implication on India's security and prosperity. Thirdly, ASEAN has a 640 million strong population with a demographic that is similar to India's, with a 35 per cent youth population and has an economy of USD 2.4 trillion. There is a tremendous growth in urbanisation and digitalisation. All these present an opportunity for India.

India engages with ASEAN at three levels—one, with ASEAN institutionally; two, with ASEAN wide initiatives, though not institutionally with ASEAN; and three, bilaterally with each member. What is important is that the instruments that India has to deal with countries bilaterally is much larger than the instruments that it has to deal with ASEAN. For example,

India has a defence partnership with each ASEAN country which is something it has not done institutionally.

There are some elements which need improvement. One, what India does with ASEAN will shape ASEAN's future too. Here, there is some degree of geopolitical stress, in part because of China and uncertainty of the U.S. posture in the region. There is a degree of fraying in unity and consensus. Therefore, the presence of the 10 leaders of each of the ASEAN countries at India's Republic Day celebrations was a tremendous signal, not just to ASEAN, but the world, of the importance that India attaches to ASEAN. Our message of ASEAN unity and centrality in a stable regional order is important and needs to be repeatedly stressed. Indian thinking is more aligned with ASEAN approach on the regional order and architecture than of major powers, which are seeking to use ASEAN and bilateral relations to advance their own geopolitical interests. Two, India needs to work and support the ASEAN way for the security architecture. Three, this can be done through joint exercises, something that Singapore hinted at as well. Four, India does not work with ASEAN, operationally, on counter-terrorism and counter radicalisation, which we must. Cyber security will also emerge as a major and important area. Five, India can improve economic engagement. Despite having the maximum number of Free Trade Agreements with the region, India's trade balance has worsened. We need to remain engaged on Regional Comprehensive Economic Partnership (RCEP), if we intend to be a serious player in the ASEAN region and beyond. We can seek terms of agreement that advance our interests and protect our sensitive areas and get a balanced and comprehensive agreement, covering goods, services and investments. Seven, India's aspirations lie in the mobility of people and there is much work to be done in this area, but it will be difficult due to ASEAN's own internal situation and demography. Eight, Indian firms have to look to export aggressively to ASEAN and India must work more on connectivity. Nine, India has to work on role of states. For example, northeast India can effectively connect with many ASEAN nations. Ten, India should replicate its successes in e-governance and financial inclusion in the ASEAN region as there is tremendous opportunity and demand there.

Finally, India has a six million strong diaspora which are playing a major role in being a bridge in Southeast Asia. But care needs to be exercised as to how this diaspora is to be used. We should not use it to influence domestic politics in these countries, as some are attempting, but as a source that reinforces the relations. India has to recognise that the diaspora will be a strong partner in strengthening India-ASEAN relations. Further, we should reclaim the heritage of our ancient links to the region to contest claims of exclusive historical links that underpin some connectivity initiatives, and use that as the foundation to build our modern partnership. In this context, it is important not to convey the impression of cultural colonisation, but speak of shared heritage, as Southeast Asia, too, has nurtured and enriched the common cultural heritage.

# 25

## Look East to Act East

*Dhruva Jaishankar*

There is a great deal of talk in India and abroad related to a number of terms that are bandied about quite frequently in the press and in commentary. This includes India's Act East policy (previously known as Look East), the Indo-Pacific, and the Quad. I will provide some context to these terms and will also try to connect some of the dots, because Southeast Asia is a very broad region with sometimes many conflicting dynamics.

If we look back over the past 70 years of India's independence, one of the things we often forget about now is that when India became independent in 1947 it found itself a natural leader in Asia, despite the effect of Partition and the myriad economic and other problems it faced at that time. India was at the vanguard of global decolonisation and had many mature democratic institutions. Within a span of three years it was able to promulgate a constitution in 1950 that provided for universal suffrage. And so, much of the rest of the world emerging from the ashes of World War II, particularly the developing world outside the United States and Europe, actually looked to India for leadership. In February and March of 1947, the Indian National Congress at that time organised a conference in Delhi. Leaders from across the region attended, including from Turkey, Iran, Indonesia, Vietnam, Australia, New Zealand, Japan, South Korea, China and Tibet.

In 1950, India was the link between the United States and the People's Republic of China in the run up to the Korean War. And India was also involved in the repatriation of prisoners of war between North and South Korea. Today, if one were to visit the Korean War Memorial in Seoul, the

Indian flag flying in front of it is a testament to India's contributions. India again was instrumental in bringing China into the community of nations, at a time when there was a lot of resistance in Asia to Communist China. India helped to facilitate the same in 1955 by extending an invitation to China to the Bandung Conference, over the objections of many other countries, including the host Indonesia. Similarly, it was India that helped facilitate Japan's re-entry into the international community after World War II. India was the first country that agreed to receive Official Development Assistance (ODA) from Japan, a project started by Japan in 1954 after it signed the Colombo Plan. At that time, many countries refused to accept ODA as the wounds of World War II were still very fresh. This was remembered by the grandson of then Prime Minister Kishi of Japan, who is now Prime Minister Abe of Japan. Of course, much of India's leadership role came crashing down after its ignominious defeat in the 1962 war with China, and many of the miscalculations and mistakes that were made in the run up to that war.

From 1962, roughly to the early 1990s, India took up a much more inward position and focused very much on the immediate neighbourhood. Indian intervention against Pakistani genocide in its East Wing led to the formation of a new nation, Bangladesh in 1971. Indian intervention also took place in the Indian Ocean, in various actions in Sri Lanka, Maldives, Mauritius and Seychelles. But basically, India did not extend itself beyond this immediate neighbourhood and the Indian Ocean, either in military or economic terms. And the currency of power in Asia really became growth, led initially by Japan; then by the four Asian Tigers South Korea, Hong Kong, Singapore and Taiwan; and then eventually by Mainland China, starting with the Deng Xiaoping's reforms in the early 1980s. We see a conception of Asia that started to take shape between the mid-1960s and the late 1980s that left no space for India. In the consciousness of the people of this region, India was often ignored, as the Indian economy did not play a meaningful role.

The circumstances started to change in the early 1990s after the end of the Cold War and the beginning of India's economic liberalisation. And we had the dawn of what was called India's Look East policy, which initially had a very explicit economic objective. It recognised that that there was a certain economic dynamism in Asia. And so India's then Prime Minister P.V. Narasimha Rao went to South Korea, Thailand, Singapore and to China, in large part to seek economic development and also seek models for inspiration for India's economic trajectory. One of the immediate and very quick successes of this Look East policy was India's institutional integration into Asia. So in the mid-1990s India joined the ASEAN Regional Forum and subsequently joined what became the East Asia Summit and then eventually the ADMM plus, the Defence Minister's Dialogue. And so India became with the exception of APEC, quite well integrated into the institutional architecture of Asia. That, to some degree is a testament to the success of India's Look East policy.

In the early 2000s, the regional dynamic started to take on a slightly different view and this was largely related to the rise of China. Undoubtedly, China's economic trajectory has been a pace setter and an inspiration, as this has lifted the largest number of people out of poverty in history. There is a lot that India and indeed the world can learn from that experience. While many countries have directly or indirectly benefited from China's economic rise, it has also been accompanied by a few characteristics which give cause for concern. China's leadership has become more centralised, its governance structures have become more opaque and its economic policies including international economic policies have become more predatory, in the form of the Belt and Road Initiative. When it comes to its territorial disputes, China has become more assertive and revisionist, be it in the South China Sea, or the airspace in the East China Sea or whether on land in the Himalayas on its border with India and Bhutan. When we consider well-established international norms on nonproliferation, on freedom of navigation or on cyber security we see China in regular violation of all of these often to the detriment of Indian security.

Not just India, but many countries around the region have started to face this dilemma. There are benefits to varying degrees from China's economic growth, prosperity, and dynamism. But these are accompanied by grave and increasing concerns about the implications of a dominant China in Asia. It is in this context that India's Look East policy transitioned into the Act East policy under Prime Minister Modi. This policy signals three things:

One, it moves beyond economics to a more comprehensive engagement including particularly on security. Two, it widens the scope from initially Southeast Asia and Northeast Asia to a much broader canvas of what we might think of as the Indo-Pacific. Three, it provides urgency to certain actionable items on the agenda. This is what differentiates the Act East policy from its previous incarnation as Look East policy: greater security, a wider scope, and greater urgency. The purpose of the Act East policy, even if it is not always explicitly so stated, is to preserve a favourable balance of power in the Indo-Pacific region.

Now what exactly do we mean by the Indo-Pacific, a term much articulated in recent years by government officials from India, Japan, the United States and from Australia? To some degree, there are variances in what is meant by the term. There are differences for example over the exact geographical scope. For Australia, the Indo-Pacific basically refers to its maritime periphery. It has an Indian Ocean and a Pacific Ocean coast. For the United States, as explicitly stated in the recently released National Security Strategy, the Indo-Pacific runs from the West coast of India to the West coast of the United States. For Japan it's a much more expansive canvas covering two entire oceans the Indian and Pacific oceans and two entire continents of Asia and Africa. India has not yet articulated the geographical boundaries of the term, but it is clear from Prime Minister Modi's own travels, if nothing else, that it extends from the East coast of Africa, the entirety of the Indian Ocean and the Western and Southern Pacific Oceans.

Despite these differences over the geographical scope of what exactly is meant by the term, there are at least three areas of convergence between these four countries' visions of the Indo-Pacific. One, it is a recognition that the Indian and Pacific Oceans form a singular strategic space. What happens in one of those oceans matters to the other. And so, what happens in the South China Sea matters for India. Similarly, what happens in the Indian Ocean matters to Japan. Two, it is a recognition that the future security and commercial dynamics will play out in the maritime space more than on land. And by defining the region by the oceans rather than the landmass is a clear indication of the priority. For India, this means achieving a greater focus not only on maritime trade including port infrastructure but also on naval capabilities. Three, despite the fact that the "Indo," in Indo-Pacific refers to the ocean and not the country of India, there really cannot be an Indo-Pacific without India in the mix. India is the largest economy in the Indian Ocean and is the largest country geographically at the centre of the Indian Ocean Region. Therefore, there is an implicit recognition that India is a balancer in the Indo-Pacific. And when President Donald Trump, in his speech in Vietnam says we are in the Indo-Pacific region, it is an implicit recognition that India features somewhere in that balance of power.

What does Acting East to preserve a favourable balance in the Indo-Pacific look like in practice? I would say the four essential elements to this, from an Indian perspective, are as follows:

One, it will mean playing a more active role in ensuring that security competition is dampened in the Indian Ocean. We are already seeing China playing a role including increasingly a military role in the Indian Ocean. They have their first overseas military base in Djibouti. There is an expectation that there will be a second base. There are other infrastructure facilities including in Sri Lanka, Kenya, Tanzania and other places which are nominally civilian in nature but going by past patterns there's always a possibility that they could be used for naval purposes as well or dual use purposes. So India needs to ensure that the security competition in this region does not adversely affect Indian interests and to do this, India is establishing in some ways its own network of military infrastructure across the region including in Seychelles and Mauritius. India is also entering into agreements to access military facilities including with Singapore, the United States, France, Oman, Japan, and with other countries across the Indian Ocean. It also has significant bilateral and multilateral arrangements for monitoring developments in this region including regular patrols in the exclusive economic zone of Seychelles and Mauritius and multilateral facilities to improve maritime domain awareness. We now also see Indian infrastructure and investment and humanitarian assistance across the region, whether from Bangladesh to Sri Lanka or from Maldives to East Africa. In the last one year itself, about 8 billion dollars in lines of credit have been extended by the Indian EXIM Bank across the world, a very large proportion of which is in the Indian Ocean Region. About a billion dollars of aid has again been granted, primarily in South Asia. We now have reinvigorated new mechanisms for governance including the Indian Ocean Rim Association (IORA) and the Bay of Bengal Initiative for Multi-Sectoral Technical and Economic Cooperation (BIMSTEC). So these regionalism and greater regionalism groupings, provision of humanitarian assistance and disaster relief efforts, greater assistance and diplomatic aid, and diplomatic attention are all parts of ensuring that the Indian Ocean does not become a region of heightened security competition.

The second element is engagement with ASEAN and the ASEAN member states both bilaterally and multilaterally and this is partly what the India-ASEAN Summit was about. We have been seeing greater pressures on ASEAN which grew in very unusual circumstances. ASEAN really evolved between the 1960s and 1990s at a time when most of the great powers were distracted or not really asserting themselves in this region and so ASEAN grew in a relative vacuum. This led to a situation where the small powers in Asia are the institutional leaders not the major powers which is very unlike most other regions of the world. We are now seeing in some ways, the reassertion of the major powers in Asia—China first and foremost, the United States, India, Japan and others, which have imposed increasing pressures on ASEAN. India's own objectives are, however, not antithetical to ASEAN centrality and to that end, India provides various kinds of economic, military and security assistance to several ASEAN countries. It provides land for the Singaporean armed forces to do exercises and provides technical assistance to the Myanmar Armed Forces. It provides training to the Vietnamese military and it does joint patrols with and coordinates patrols with the Thai armed forces in the Andaman Sea. So these are just a few examples of some of the ways in which India is providing some assistance and cooperating with the Southeast Asian militaries. A caveat here is in order as one area that has not been going so well for India is its economic integration with Southeast Asia. Trade remains relatively slow growing and connectivity by land, by air and even sea remains weak. And so a lot more needs to be done by India to play the role of an economic balancer. India is but the ninth largest trade partner of ASEAN which is below Hong Kong and Taiwan. So ASEAN engagement is the second important element to Acting East.

The third important element is deepening security partnerships with likeminded maritime powers in the region. The three of utmost importance are the United States, Japan and Australia. India has been doing a lot with all three countries in terms of deepening its defence partnerships, the most with the US, followed by Japan, and thereafter with Australia. There has been a lot of movement on bilateral and trilateral engagements and now there is increasing talk for the first time on quadrilateral cooperation amongst these countries. This extends to joint exercises to improve inter-operability, as also staff talks and dialogues at the bureaucratic and political level to exchange views on issues. With the United States so far, it also includes some capacity building efforts. This may also extend eventually to Japan and Australia as well. So we are seeing in some ways these four countries again either bilaterally or trilaterally working together now in different contexts. A lot has been made of the quadrilateral dialogue but I want to insert a few notes of caution. There have been a few meetings by relatively junior officials from the foreign ministries or external affairs ministries of the four countries in 2017 and nothing more than that. So this represents only a very exploratory effort to see where there are potential areas of cooperation involving these four countries. The defence ministries are not yet involved and so it is still premature to talk about there being any commitments or any kind of regular exercises involving all four countries together. The agenda still needs to be worked out. That being said, the very fact that for the first time in 10 years these four countries have met together at the official level is a significant event and accordingly has received a lot of attention in the Indian and international media.

The fourth and final element of Acting East involves maintaining a good and stable relationship with China and this is going to be increasingly difficult. We have seen Chinese assertiveness on the India-China border and there is a huge trade imbalance between the two countries. Chinese support to Pakistan runs counter to Indian interests and sensitivities. Managing this bilateral relationship whether through a more determined defence posture on the border, or by boycotting the Belt and Road forum as India did in 2017, or also by keeping open lines of engagement and dialogue will be important and will be a very tricky balance in the years ahead.

# 26

## India and Indonesia

*Pradeep Rawat*

Indonesia is important because it is the largest country in Southeast Asia, the biggest in terms of population and has the largest economy. Geographically, it is strategically placed, as any ship coming from the Pacific to the Indian Ocean or the South China Sea has to pass through straits which are contiguous to the Indonesian island. It is also an important member of ASEAN. It is a resource rich country with timber, oil, coal and spices. It has a young population that can see its demographic dividend.

Coming to society, the values that Indonesia espouses are important. For example, while they do not use the word tolerance, they accept differences. They are highly diverse with 700 languages, multiple islands with different religions, like Christianity, Hinduism and Islam living in harmony. Indonesia has multiple linkages with India. It is our maritime neighbour—the western-most tip of Sumatra Island is only 90 nautical miles from the Andamans. We share deep cultural similarities with the Ramayana and Mahabharata being very popular. Even the name "Indonesia" itself means 'islands of India'. In terms of trade, India has always traded with Indonesia historically. Today, Indonesia is India's largest trading partner in Southeast Asia. India's investment in Indonesia is USD 15 billion, that is second only behind Singapore. Our Bilateral trade between the two countries amounts to USD 17 billion. India is among the largest importers of crude palm oil and coal from Indonesia. The Indian diaspora is very old in Indonesia and in fact, during Ramadan you will find locals eating *khichdi.* The new wave of migrating Indians are businessmen and entrepreneurs in the service sector. The Indian diaspora now numbers around 100,000 people. Indian diaspora is highly regarded.

Both India and Indonesia are 'chaotic,' active democratic countries. Other shared values are rule of law and unity in diversity. Because of these shared values and connectivity, Indonesia is very important for India to create a new rule-based security architecture. Both countries can play a very important role in evolving this architecture and strengthening IORA and Act East Policy. Engagement with Indonesia has intensified in the last few years. In January 2018 alone, the Indian External Affairs Minister visited Indonesia, the Indonesian Defence Minister visited India, the first ever strategic dialogue at the NSA level took place and the Indonesian President visited India for the ASEAN Summit. This indicates a clear will from both sides to further enhance engagement with each other.

# 27

# India's Relations with Israel, Iran and Palestine

*Arun K Singh*

India has a very interesting but very complex relationships with Israel, Palestine and Iran. Among these, perhaps the most complex and interesting relationship for India to handle is with Israel. When Israel was established in 1948 and there was a vote at the UN to create the state of Israel, India voted against the establishment of the state of Israel. This had its origins in India's own struggle for national independence, where the leaders of the mainstream movement for national independence had fought for creation of a state which would be a secular inclusive state and not one based on religion. As India had opposed the creation of Pakistan, which was being created on the basis of religion, then consistency dictated that India should oppose the creation of all states that were being created based on religion. India's vote against the creation of the state of Israel was, hence one based on this principle, but it did not signify any anti-Semitism stance and that is a fact that is well recognised. There has never been any discrimination against Jewish people in the entire course of Indian history and that is something which the Israelis value. Consequently, whenever there is any major event hosted by the Indian origin Jewish community in Israel, they would fly an Indian flag along with the Israeli flag—something very unusual because most Jewish communities who have migrated to Israel have migrated on the basis of the push factor and so they dissociate themselves from the countries where they lived earlier.

It is only the Indian origin Jewish community and to some extent the US origin Jewish community that continues to associate with their country of origin. During the holocaust against Jews in Europe in the second world war, many of the Jews came from Europe to India to survive. Here, they were welcomed and found a home to be in. And they lived here for some years and then moved on to Israel and they all remember that. So although India voted against the establishment of the state of Israel, it accorded recognition to the state of Israel in 1950, based on the facts on the ground because the state had been created. Soon after that, there was an attempt in India to also establish full diplomatic relations with Israel but that did not happen at that time and got delayed. The reason was that post-independence, a large number of Muslims from India had moved over to Pakistan, but a significant number, about one-third of the Muslim population chose to stay back. And there was a concern in the government that if India was seen to be taking a pro-Israeli position, it could adversely impact on this population. There is also the argument that India wanted the support of the Arab world in the UN on the issue of J&K. Also, the attack on the Suez canal in 1956, by the UK and France along with Israel, queered the pitch for India. This was followed by the 1967 and 1973 Arab-Israeli wars which further stalled the establishment of full diplomatic relations. The short point being made is that foreign policy choices, while being made on the basis of national interest are also impacted by global developments. Eventually, it was only in 1992 that full diplomatic relations were established between India and Israel. This was the period which saw the dissolution of the USSR and the end of the Cold War. Also, in 1988, the Oslo peace process had started between Israel and Palestine, and as the Palestinians themselves were moving towards establishing some kind of agreements with Israel, there was nothing now to hold India back. In the period 1991–92, a large number of countries in the world started establishing full diplomatic relations with Israel, including Russia and China and so did India too.

Even while India did not have full diplomatic relations with Israel, there was a lot going on between the two countries which enabled India to take the relationship to another level. It was Israel which provided military assistance to India in the period 1962–71. It was done quietly then, but now is a matter of public record and this was helpful to India. There was also a presence in Israel of a strong Indian origin community in the diamond business. Even today, the Israeli diamond bourse is a very strong part of the global trade in diamonds of which about 10 per cent of the trade is generated by Indian origin persons and Indian origin companies which have been present in Israel since the 60s, much before the establishment of diplomatic relations.

Since the establishment of diplomatic relations with Israel, ties in different areas have strengthened of which defence is an important component. India has moved beyond just a buyer–seller relationship to development of technologies, where both sides have worked to jointly develop short and medium range surface to air missiles. Today, a significant part of India's defence imports come from Israel and Israel has become the fourth major defence partner of India along with the US, Russia and France.

So Israel is important to India as India is important for Israel. Another area of focus is the people to people dimension. There are 80,000 Indian origin Jewish people in Israel comprising of four different communities, one each from Mumbai area, Cochin, Kolkata and more recently, there is a new community from Mizoram. Interestingly, when this group of people were living in India, they were considered technically by the Jewish agencies and others as part of the Jewish diaspora. Now that they are living in Israel, India considers them as part of the Indian diaspora, which gives India another basis to consolidate the India–Israel relationship.

During Prime Minister Narendra Modi's visit to Israel in 2017, water and agriculture were identified as strategic areas of cooperation between the two countries. Israel has great strength in water technologies and in agriculture. I went to a kibbutz in Israel's north and I saw how, in their greenhouse technologies they were producing top quality lychees and mangoes. As of now, Israel has set up 22 centres of excellence in India. While earlier there was a bit of diffidence at the political level, the substantive cooperation was progressing well. Today, the optics and the politics of the relationship have changed since 2014, especially with the first ever Prime Ministerial visit of India to Israel, which was followed six months later by a visit of the Israeli Premier to India. This kind of relationship had never developed earlier and is truly transformational, beyond the substantive cooperation.

## India's Relations with Iran

In 1996, India had shut her embassy in Kabul, when the Taliban seized power in the country. The only Indian access then was in the Northern part of Afghanistan where Ahmed Shah Masood and his forces were active. We were also running a field hospital in Tajikistan's Farkhor area. The Taliban fled Kabul on 13 November 2001 and with the eviction of the Taliban, the Indian government decided to reopen its embassy in Kabul and reestablish Indian presence. It was still a warlike situation in Afghanistan, there was no government and fighting was still going on. Overflying Pakistan was not an option as Pakistan would have denied permission, so the only way to get there was via Iran. We took approval of the American authorities because they controlled the air space, and Iran gave approval on short notice, which enabled the Indian embassy to be reestablished by November 20 and start humanitarian assistance. Iran, therefore remains critical for India in terms of access to Afghanistan and to Central Asia. India is also working on a North-South corridor, and if it develops well, it will enable movement from an Indian port to an Iranian port, thence through Iran to the Caspian Sea and into Russia and beyond, which will provide far better access to Russia and Eastern Europe.

For strategic reasons, Iran remains an extremely important partner for India. A significant portion of India's energy imports also come from Iran, which in 2017 was India's third biggest oil supplier after Iraq and Saudi Arabia. Now in the antagonistic dynamic that we see of the Israel–Iran relationship there are also issues related to Pakistan and Afghanistan at one end and the United States at the other that India has to be mindful of. Pakistan has always been nervous of India's relationship with Israel and if India improves its relations with the US, there will be a play on some of the other relationships, especially as the US–Iran relationship is a very complicated one.

The US–Iran relationship is strained, because of the unsavoury memories of 1979 when the Americans were driven out of Iran and hostages were taken in their embassy and also because of Israeli anxieties with respect to Iran. Israel believes that Iran's nuclear programme is an existential threat to Israel, as a result of which Israel mounts a global and regional effort to mobilise against Iran and to have policies adopted in the US targeting some of the developments in Iran. Of late, President Trump has said that he will not certify the Iran nuclear deal in the future which will open up a host of new complications. And if the US goes back to sanctioning Iran, then India may have to comply, because the companies and the banks who would otherwise have been trading with Iran could be sanctioned by the US, and the India–US trade and economic relationship is far more important to many of the companies than the India–Iran trade and economic relationship. How this plays out and how India handles the situation will have to be seen.

Israel is a gateway to the US, but only up to a point. At a time when the US was not able to partner with India in defence cooperation, Israel was doing so and at competitive cost and acceptable levels of technology. But now the US itself is partnering with India. The role of the Jewish diaspora also gains significance. The Jewish community in the US has significant influence and is very encouraged about the US–India relationship, especially when it sees the India–Israel relationship evolving in a positive direction. As a result, when there were difficulties in the US Congress over the India–US Civil Nuclear Deal, at the time of President Bush in 2006, 2007, 2008, the Jewish community in the US had stepped up to help India. In 2016, when the Obama administration decided to supply F-16 aircraft to Pakistan and India lobbied against this decision in the US Congress, again the Jewish community in the US was helpful to India. So this is the additional dimension that India can leverage.

The question arises, as to the extent to which India's and Iran's interests align over Afghanistan, as despite sectarian differences, Iran has now reached out to the Taliban. Now, when the Taliban was in power, India and Iran along with Russia and Uzbekistan had worked very closely together before 9/11 in the framework of supporting the Northern Alliance. At that time, the Taliban were controlling almost 90 per cent of Afghanistan and only 10 per cent was held together by the Northern Alliance. Both Iran and Russia were hostile to the Taliban as their interests were affected. Iranian diplomats had been killed in Mazar-e-Sharif and Russia was wary of the Taliban because of the possibility of terrorists entering Central Asia and thence into Russia through the northern border of Afghanistan. And certainly it was also contrary to Uzbek interests. However, as global interests are never constant, post the ouster of the Taliban, the only country which is comfortable with the continued US presence in Afghanistan, other than Afghanistan itself is India, especially because India has invested heavily in building infrastructure in Afghanistan, the assistance amounting to over USD 2 billion. This assistance has had a tremendous impact on the local population, and India today remains the most popular country in Afghanistan. But India has been able to provide this assistance within the overall security framework provided by the United States. Sans that framework, Afghanistan could descend into violence and instability. Post 9/11 Iran initially offered to help the US as their interests and Taliban interests were not coinciding and Iran allowed US aircraft overflights over Iranian territory during the conduct of the war in 2001. Unfortunately, President Bush in his State of the Union Address in 2003 described Iran as one of the axis of evil. And that really put pressure on Iranian leaders and the US–Iran relationship deteriorated over time and Iran is once again faced with the prospect of being sanctioned by the US. They thus obviously do not want US presence in Afghanistan. Similarly, Russia too is not comfortable with US presence in Afghanistan, which explains their approach to the Taliban. For India, Iran remains critical in terms of supplies to Afghanistan. But in terms of regional and global policy around Afghanistan, there is a lack of convergence at this stage.

Before the Iran nuclear deal called the JCPOA (Joint Comprehensive Plan of Action) was signed, the US had imposed sanctions, and supplies from Iran had to be progressively brought down. At that time, India was in deep conversation with the US government and they were helpful and enabled India to avoid the sanctions as they too were looking at the India–US relationship. And while the US had a requirement in law that the imports be brought down, they understood many of the difficulties and challenges that India faced and gave India flexibility on the margin. Without the use of Iranian ports, India would not be in a position to continue its development activities in Afghanistan, which would have hurt US interests. So, in the US legislation, there was a provision to cater for this requirement. Diplomacy thus requires the ability to work one's way through contradictory situations.

## Palestine

In World War I, Indian soldiers took part in the liberation of Haifa, but at that time it was to drive out the Ottoman Empire. Later, in the context of India's own national movement for independence, India argued for a state to be established but not on the basis of religion. India sustained that principled position even as it moved ahead with the recognition of Israel in 1950. But India had to be mindful of Muslim sentiment both within the country as also in the wider region of South Asia, West Asia and Southeast Asia. India thus continued to maintain a strong relationship with Palestine and in 1974, was the first non-Arab country to recognise the PLO led by Yasser Arafat as the sole representative of the Palestinian people. This was significant as it meant that any negotiation with Israel had to be done only by the PLO. In 1988 India recognised the state of Palestine before most other countries and in 1996, established a representative office, first in Gaza where Arafat was based and then later moved to Ramallah in 2003, when Arafat moved there because of some of the challenges in Gaza. Today, India's representative office continues to function from Ramallah and India provides economic assistance to the Palestinian Authority and the Palestinian people. India supports a two-state solution to the problem in Palestine, with separate capitals, and the capital of each state to be negotiated between the two parties concerned. That is the basis on which India is currently moving forward. It is because India has a principled position on Palestine that it is able to move forward in its relations with Israel, in conformity with India's national interest.

Today, India has very close cooperation with Israel. This poses challenges in dealing with contradictory requirements, as India has excellent relations with Palestine, Iran and also with the Arab countries in the Gulf. Prime Minister Modi has visited several of those countries, and will also be visiting Oman, UAE and Palestine. So India is working to strengthen our relations with both sides. Iran refuses to recognise the existence of Israel, and the latter looks upon the former as an existential threat, but many of the Arab states have softened their position on Israel. Back channel talks have been reported between Saudi Arabia and Israel, and for a long time Israel has had a trade office in Qatar, and Jordan and Egypt have full diplomatic relations with Israel. The softening of the Arab states towards Israel has much to do with their own antagonism towards Iran and Israel is building on that to create equations that could serve its interests.

India must continue to work on building its relations with each of these countries on a bilateral basis and see that its relationships are not held hostage to conflicting positions adopted by different countries in the region, based on their own perceived national interest. International relations can never be an either/or situation. For example, most countries that have good relations with India also have relations with Pakistan. Russia has excellent historical relationship with India but is also now trying to build relations with Pakistan. Similarly, nothing can prevent India from building our bilateral relations with countries in our national interest even if those countries have problems with each other. That is the approach that India is following.

# INDIA AND THE WORLD

# 28

## India-US Relations

*Ashok Malik*

My focus on the India-US relationship is on five potential problem areas. These are tactical problem areas and none of them is a potential relationship breaker. The future remains smooth and will expand, but these five problem areas will keep coming back in some form or the other.

First is the issue of trade. The Trump administration and before that the Obama administration, began a gentle move away from the liberal trade model. One of the biggest gainers of the liberal trade model was China, but India gained too. The shift, therefore, is of concern to India, though its impact on China will be far greater.

This has led to a deeper question. US engagement with India on defence, especially in the Indo-Pacific region, has enhanced, and also the discussion on a Quad kind of relationship. When viewed in the context of the next two to three years, this is fine, but five to six years down the line, when US presence in the Indo-Pacific is stronger, would there be an accrual of economic interests to India along with the enhanced defence relationship? In a sense, the US will have to come back to a freer trade model. India will wait for that model and its mechanism and see whether it brings benefits or problems to India.

Second, the US, like many other countries, has become protectionist. India and the US are mirror images of each other in terms of trade and economic vision. Though the US has an economy many times the size of India's economy, fundamentally, both nations are similar, in that both are trying to leverage a local market through international investments. So, if you access Indian markets you have to go for "Make in India". President Obama's policy was on similar lines, stated politely. President Trump is saying the same thing in a more blunt and forthright manner. This means that both India and the US want access to the other's markets while protecting their own. This is the fundamental paradox and is also a threat. Also, if you look at the nature of the US and Indian economies, both are dependent on services. Both are also looking at robust enhancement of manufacturing capacity, not at the lower end, because we lost that to China, but in terms of knowledge like the pharma industry, where both countries compete. Or in terms of precision manufacture, space technology where India provides cheaper options as compared to the US, and also Internet companies. Europe does not have Internet companies like India—it has no Amazon, Uber and so on. And China has shut off the world. India has a home-grown e-commerce ecosystem and it has to grow it by being open to the international investment as well as compete with US competitiveness and survive.

There is also the matter of the Indian diaspora and liberal immigration. The Trump administration has tightened the norms for issuing new H-1B visa applicants in line with its goal to protect American workers from discrimination and replacement by foreign labour. The H-1B visa allows US employers to temporarily employ foreign workers in specialty occupations. This issue was under discussion since the Bush administration and is a legacy of the 1990s boom. Once the boom ended, the system started coming under pressure and the debate is now between more jobs for US citizens or a liberal trade order. The impact is severe for India as it leads the pack when it comes to allotment of H-1B visas. There is a human bridge in the form of Indian diaspora, and millions of middle class families in India have a stake in the US because a member is working there. The people-to-people link is fundamental to this relationship and precedes the government-to-government link. There is an idea that this human bridge can be replaced by shared perceptions of the common threat faced from China and Islamism. I don't think that is possible.

Third is the way India and the US look at Iran and the Middle East. India and the US have looked at Iran and Pakistan as mirror images. US looks at Pakistan as located at a very strategic geographic location and India does the same with Iran. While India and the US are increasingly on the same page on issues concerning Pakistan, there is divergence with respect to Iran. For India's Central Asia and Afghanistan policy, Iran is an important link. The US views Iran as a destabilising influence, due to its nuclear programme and support to

Hezbollah. In the Middle East, the US would rather play the Sunni card than balance the Sunni-Shia divide playing out between Riyadh and Teheran, and is clearly working on isolating Iran. India is not comfortable with that as its relations with Iran are vital as a link to Afghanistan and Central Asia and also for its energy requirements. India is also aware that it will be the largest importer of oil from the Middle East in the next decade, even more than China.

The fourth area of concern is that three of the last four US Presidents have flirted with the idea of a compact with China. After India's Pokhran test, President Clinton spoke about using China to stabilise South Asia. Obama, during his Presidency, spoke about the G2 world. President Trump, in the early months of his Presidency, spoke about working with China. The only US president who has not spoken on these lines is President Bush.

Fifth, Indians are bewildered with US obsession with Russia. India's relations with Russia are not as they used to be in the Cold War days, and today the economic relationship is limited. India is no longer solely dependent on Russia for the purchase of weapon systems, though Russia is still a major arms supplier to India. Besides purchase of arms, there is hardly any economic engagement with Russia. And we do not see too many tourists or students going to Russia. But US obsession with Russia bewilders India and it seems like a Cold War overhang. The US seems obsessed with Russian attacks on US systems, which may well be true, but is silent on the many attacks from the Chinese to fracture the Internet, which is a global concern. Even Hollywood appears to be happier making retro-Cold War movies, showcasing Russia as the all-time enemy, but does not show the same zeal when it comes to China. Much is written in the US about the Russian mafia—the more insidious network in American academia, politics, business, and think tanks that China has established in US has layers and layers to it, but is hardly ever mentioned. Sometimes one wonders if America is looking at the wrong enemy.

# 29

## India, Latin America and the Caribbean

*Dattesh Parulekar*

As a geopolitical construct, Latin America is a term, used, to connote the 20 sovereign constituents, straddling the Western Hemisphere, which comprise, what we routinely in geographical terms, comprehend and aver, as 'Central' (seven) and 'South' (thirteen) America. However, in India's strategic calculus, the region, though distinct, has found itself sweepingly clubbed, with the adjoining Caribbean region, with its loose skein of 13 islands countries, strewn across the Caribbean Sea and the Atlantic Ocean, to constitute, what the Ministry of External Affairs, of the Government of India, perfunctorily dubs, as the Latin American and Caribbean (LAC) region. The composite region of LAC, hems-in a populace, in excess of six hundred million, embodying a rising middle class, and a younger work-force, and which, despite its predominantly primary commodities-based production hue, has exuded relative economic resilience, that has witnessed the region's economies, accretion themselves, in the vicinity of 3-4 per cent annualised growth, over much of this century.

The region, harking back into history, manifested a colonial patchwork of the multitude of European imperial powers of yore. Nevertheless, it was overwhelmingly under the tutelage of the Spanish (virtually all of Central and South America) and the Portuguese (Brazil), with circumscribed influence of the French and the Dutch, and with the British sway sweeping across much of the Caribbean. These countries have been independent for close to two centuries barring the exception of Cuba. India's relations with the region and most of its constituents, particularly those of Iberian colonial heritage, remained notional and stunted. For New Delhi, the Latin American region represented a political backwater, firmly ensconced within the American strategic orbit, during the breadth of the bipolar Cold War, with its yawning geographical detachment, and linguistic and cultural divergence, further accentuating the sense of being removed from each other, notwithstanding the literary contacts that existed between celebrated, luminous exponents, at either end. Whatever little coordination and convergence was in evidence, became possible on account of solidarist notions of South-South cooperation, in the context of the riven North-South axis, over trade and development issues, pursued through the aegis and auspices of the agency of the United Nations Conference on Trade and Development (UNCTAD).

With Latin America oscillating, between intermittent periods of democracy, interspersed, with substantive epochs of praetorian military dictatorships and authoritarian regimes, and smitten, by the Raul Prebisch enjoined economic philosophical moorings of Import-Substitution Industrialisation (ISI), and India, for its part, steeped in the socialist mixed economic model delivering anaemic growth, the context and rationale for material mutual cooperation failed to beckon beyond sporadic instances, blighted by the visible commonality of their economic production content-configuration and structures, rather than being complementary to each other.

The demise of the bipolar schema in world affairs, brought on a tectonically transformed concourse of circumstances, within which to forge a new framework and template for India-Latin America ties. While India had unshackled the labyrinthine fetters on its centrally planned command economy, and wittingly embraced the trinity of economic liberalisation, privatisation and globalisation, precipitating the commenced pursuit of a veritably global foreign policy based on diversified diplomatic engagement and interchange, the region of Latin America emerged as an inclined juxtaposing counterpart, with its countries emerging out of the despairing decade of the 1980s, proverbially termed as the "Lost Decade," putatively marked by profound hyper-inflation and the spiralling mire of public-debt, not to mention these sovereigns turning their backs on military dispensations and opting for predilections in entrenching constitutional and popular democracies, as exemplified and borne-out in 21st century Chile, for instance.

Even as Washington's fetish for the region subsided, its vice like grip over the region's economic fortunes wasn't ready to yield just yet, anchored and emanating in the 'Washington Consensus' phalanx of neo-liberal economic prescriptions, that were forthcoming, from the portals of the Bretton Woods institutional firmament, of the IMF and the World Bank, putting a premium on macro-economic stabilisation and management, trade and investment liberalisation, and ordaining an expanded role for market forces, bringing undulating trajectories of economic growth and imbalanced development, amidst widening socio-economic inequalities and exacerbating income-disparities. Yet, on the whole, the United States strategically retreated from the region, a vacuum that is abhorred in the realm of international statecraft, and the space of which has since been progressively consumed by a surging China and a resurgent Russia. The overweening US covert action in engineering the coup that sought to depose military fatigues man turned populist Communist leader Hugo Chavez in oil verdant Venezuela, sullied Washington's image across the region, with its action seen as an unsavoury throwback to the Reagan era surreptitious shenanigans and the clandestine sleight-of-hand operations, dating back through the decades of the Cold War.

This said, the scope and tenor of India-Latin America and Caribbean (LAC) region trade has traversed a long way, emerging out of its meagre sum of about USD 200 million back in 1991, to approximately USD 45 billion, currently; however, for a constellation of 33 sovereigns, this volume represents a case of being much underwhelmed, and poignantly pales in inevitable comparison with the peer power China, whose trade interchange has burgeoned exponentially with the region. Plausibly, New Delhi's trade exchanges remain circumscribed, with few product-lines, a set of countries with whom intensified relations persist, and a stereotyped conception and policy-conceptualisation of the region, that refuses to be shed by the politico-diplomatic establishment, to obvious mutual detriment. From a one-time straitjacketed view that Latin America militated under the wings of Washington, to an equally parochial notion that the region is sold-out on being suborn to Beijing, New Delhi's understanding of the complexity of the region, has been sanguinely simplistic and agonisingly superficial. There are more than handy instances, to disabuse this starry-eyed erroneous belief, of Latin America disposing, as a full-on supplicant, to the big powers in town. Back in 1994-95, it was Latin American consensus led by the proverbial France of the region, Brazil, that saw the still-born abort of the Clinton touted initiative of the Free Trade Area of the Americas (FTAA), mooted in the wake of the seminal consummation of the North

American Free Trade Agreement (NAFTA) of 1994, which incorporated Mexico from the region. In 2002, at the apogee of the Bush administration's diplomatic push to elicit a UN Security Council Resolution authorising its invasion of Iraq, it was the likes of Mexico and Chile, which despite being sentient of what punitive measures lay in store from a US administration that had shown itself to be vengeful, nevertheless, held firm against the US-UK misadventure, contributing to the diplomatic contretemps at the horse-shoe, which ultimately saw the UN process terminated, to the chagrin and consternation of Washington. Similarly, over recent years, Latin American countries have tended to band together to assert their presence as being more than just lining-up the numbers behind Washington within the OAS, as had been the norm since the institution's inception in 1948. The Latin American coalition of ALBA (Bolivarian Alliance) of Venezuela, Ecuador, Bolivia, was able to successfully galvanise support for Peruvian Caesar Gaviria's candidature against the US-sponsored candidate of the Mexican Foreign Minister Ernesto Derbez, with the latter ultimately pulling out, in favour of the former.

Latin American countries too, stand culpable, in their stereotypical view that holds India as the land of charm, mystique, intrigue, even harbouring the colonially perverse imagery perpetuated about India, of being the land of snake-charmers, primal subsisting individuals and the ilk. Its nigh that Latin American societies including those within academia, acquainted themselves with the breadth and depth of socio-economic transformations underway across India, which ought to begin with migrating away from archetypal research about socio-economic phenomenon, prevalent within antiquated India, but relics to reality. A salutary beginning to strategic understanding came by way of the Government of India's 'FOCUS LAC' initiative of the year 2000, a strategy enunciated by the Ministry of Commerce, which sought to capture its outreach to the expansive distant region of Latin America and the Caribbean, through a fifteen-point agenda, premised on an approach to five countries and across five product-lines in what could be termed the 5x5 proposition in action. Needless to state, that an overtly transactional scheme operated, as India, requiting a slew of strategic natural resource and industrially sourced raw-materials, foraged for its hydrocarbons needs from Venezuela and Ecuador, with its copper, gold, silver and attendant minerals and metals requirements sourced from Chile and Peru. Brazil being the largest country, economy and society within the LAC region, and a regional and global powerhouse in its own right, was bound to be engaged distinctly, as was precisely the case from New Delhi.

Notwithstanding what has been an incrementally growing relationship between India and the LAC region, there have been certain inflection-points, which have catalysed an upswing, in engagement. One such realm is the story around what brought the present-day footprint of Indian pharmaceuticals to the LAC region. Brazil, under then President Luiz Inacio Lula da Silva, had piloted the world's largest anti-HIV program, subsidising the provisioning of anti-retroviral drugs to its significantly afflicted sections of citizenry. Amidst a scenario where President Lula found himself held to virtual ransom by the high-handed arbitrariness of the US-based drugs majors charging prohibitively high prices for their products, Lula reached out to Prime Minister Vajpayee during his 2002 visit as India's Chief Guest for the Republic Day, inquiring whether India could step-in and supplant the US companies, should he pull the plug on them. Finding an avid India, he snapped on links with Washington and this marked the opportune moment for Indian pharma majors to foray into the region, to the point where today, they hold significant stakes across a slew of national markets in Central and South America, identifying the region as one of its promising growth markets, and even deploying localised production facilities in recent years, outpacing Chinese pharma exports to the region in the process.

Another momentous instance was the joining of India with Chile alongside the US-suggested and UN-established United Nations Democracy Fund, supporting fragile societies with civilian sector capacity building and institutional empowerment towards entrenching democracy, transparency and good governance. It's remarkable that a country such as Chile, which until 1990, was in the grips of a brutal dictatorship of Gen. Augusto Pinochet, had come so far as to be a founding member of the salutary UNDEF initiative, on the back of its sustained commitment to democracy and scrupulous constitutional handovers of civilian power, since 1990, to be seated, alongside a celebrated exemplary democracy such as India. In 2005, it was in the waning days of the Vajpayee premiership, that the 'I-B-SA' (India, Brazil, South Africa) Dialogue Forum found its inception, predicated on the considered belief that the three regional powerhouses, and emerging nations on the global horizon, could be the lynchpins to integrating three sub-regions and even continents, coalesced around developmental, human capacity building and best practices sharing framework for multilateral cooperation. As India and Brazil sustained themselves through the initial O-5 (Outreach Five) morphing into the B-R-I-C, later to be the 'B-R-I-C-S' (Brazil, Russia, India, China, and South Africa since 2010), besides, also being integral to the constitution of the G-04 clique of credible and eminent aspirants for Permanent Membership of the UN Security Council, it has implied that the relationship between New Delhi and Brasilia, has taken evident centre-stage. One recalls how, during the business-end of the process at eliciting the India-specific waiver from the IAEA, in the context of the Indo-US Civil Nuclear Agreement, Brazil was in the Chair at a crucial juncture, and disposed facilitative to the process rather than hold out on some form of impractical conditionality, or even obstructionist, as was the case with certain European countries on the matter. This, despite the fact that Brazil and Argentina moved, in the wake of the end of the Cold War, to mothball their commissioned Nuclear Programs during the early 1990s, and in the light of its own experiences and reflections, Brasilia could well have been understood, had they sought to resist India being treated exceptionally, bestowed with privileges, without signing the Nuclear Non-Proliferation Treaty (NPT). Similarly, when President Obama, pouted unequivocally on India's credentials to Permanent Membership of the UNSC, during his 2010 sojourn to India, in contrast to Tokyo and Berlin, both of whose Foreign Offices, questioned the logic of India being singled out, from within the G-04, Brazil's Itamaraty endorsed India's cogent candidature and spoke constructively about the sentiment expressed by President Obama. However, while none could deny the criticality of the India-Brazil relationship, which is truly comprehensive and genuinely multifaceted, yet it need not come at the expense of an equally productive and fully developed Indian engagement of other peer powers and sovereign entities across the transcontinental region, whether it be an Argentina from within MERCOSUR, or for that matter the four sovereign constituents within the Pacific Alliance (Mexico, Peru, Colombia and Chile), who are eminent within the Asia-Pacific scheme of things, or the lesser known mortals within them, who might not be touted, but still can contribute to many flagship priorities that India delineates for itself, from Sustainable Development to Renewable Energies, and Human Capacitation to Technology Transfer. It needs to be appreciated and appraised, that overdoing the schmooze with Brazil, can ruffle feathers in a region, where competition remains rife. Brazil is the singular Portuguese speaking country in an otherwise overwhelmingly Spanish heritage region, thereby questioning the hypothesis as to whether Brasilia can at all serve as the gateway to the region, something which excoriates from India's misplaced approach. While Prime Minister Dr. Manmohan Singh's sojourn to Brazil in 2005 was momentous in itself, given that it was the first Premier level working visit to the region since Indira Gandhi in 1967 (Prime Minister Narasimha Rao visited Brazil for the Earth Summit in Rio in 1992), yet, the stand alone visit to Brazil was in the context of the BRIC Summit. Subsequent visits by Prime Ministers have been conducted along similar lines, to specific countries, which are hosts of multilateral or plurilateral Summits, with symbolic trips left to Indian Presidents and Vice Presidents, an out of sync politico-diplomatic format.

While the India-Latin America relationship has meandered, at least politico-diplomatically, there is promise to behold since Prime Minister Modi has ascended to national helm-ship. After all, as Chief Minister of Gujarat, Mr. Modi had engaged diplomatic envoys from Latin American and Caribbean countries based out of Delhi (they go by the nomenclature of 'GRULAC'), and had even ensured that the LAC region participation at Vibrant Gujarat Summit gets a separate pavilion space to showcase their wares and shingle their proficiency. Indian foreign office mandarins and the diplomatic community from the LAC region saw such cultivation of the region by a provincial Indian politician, long before his national ascent was in the mix, as a refreshing whiff of fresh air, auguring well for ties. This stands in stark contrast with how Prime Minister Manmohan Singh, a distinguished economist, appraised the country of a visiting President, viz., Argentina, as nothing more than a living embodiment of serial 'sovereign default'; this to a country which is a major bulk producer of soya and soy-oil on the one hand and is home to huge untapped deposits of shale energy reserves, besides being a major agricultural and technological powerhouse in itself. Notwithstanding the dint of India having bailed Argentina out of its aggravating spectre during 2011-12, when in response to abrupt Chinese suspension of purchases of its soya, understood to be a punitive retaliation for Argentine moves aimed at mitigating Chinese predatory practices in the country, the South American nation, found itself staring at an agricultural disaster, had it not been for India, which, acquired the stacked-up inventory of soya in bulk, and since, both have found a reliable partner in each other.

Prime Minister Modi has enunciated as part of his Foreign Policy doctrine, the idea of "No Country Left Behind," exhorting his ministerial colleagues to ensure that they visit as many countries globally as would be requisite to their ministerial responsibilities, such that no country is shorn of an Indian ministerial sojourn, come the end of his term in office in 2019. Emphasising the scope and penetrative traction of Indian Soft Power, through his clarion-call from the bully pulpit of the UNGA in September 2014, for an International Yoga Day, it shouldn't be lost on anyone that the first set of nations, to emphatically endorse the call for such a designated day for Yoga, was none other than those from the LAC region. It should surprise none, since Yoga is not only a huge draw across most of Latin America, but that this Roman Catholic part of the world views the art and practice of Yoga, as much more than a form of aerobics, perceiving it as a holistic medium for rejuvenation of the body, mind and the soul, precisely how Yoga, ought to be comprehended, and internalised. Tied to this is the tremendous potential for Indian herbal medicine of Ayurveda to grow in popularity across the region, with some considered estimates pegging its potential to be to the tune of about USD 500 million. H.H. Sri Sri Ravishankar ji made history in Buenos Aires back in 2010, when close to five thousand Argentines congregated in the central square of the Argentine capital, to perform 'Sudarshan Kriya,' backed-up by the Prime Minister attending and addressing an Art of Living sponsored Yoga event in Buenos Aires, on the margins of the recently concluded G20 Summit in November-December 2018. Sri Sri's role in helping bringing the FARC (Revolutionary Armed Forces of Colombia) to the negotiating table and to nudge them to accept a peace deal that could bring an end to the longest running insurgency movement in living memory, by engaging them in Havana, Cuba, has been glowingly lauded by none other than the then Colombian President, Juan Manuel Santos and the FARC Supreme Leader too.

There are a multitude of factors that make India and Latin America partners in mutual fit. The LAC countries are verdantly endowed in a wide spectrum of strategic natural resources as also mono-cropped agricultural commodities, from being reposed of source raw-materials to being home to intermediate ingredients for industrial applications, all the way to holding the keys to futuristic material and frontier fuels (Bolivia accounts for 40 percent of globally sourced Lithium). With large landmasses, plentiful of water, huge grasslands and small population, they constitute propitious territory and fertile ground for India and its agro-processing companies to harness this potential towards addressing the challenge of food security. On the energy security front, Venezuela is widely believed to hold the world's largest undiscovered and yet to be tapped quantum of oil, if only it had been blessed with a modicum of sane, sagacious governance. It covets India as one of its biggest consumers. No wonder then, that despite the diplomatic frigidity between Washington and Caracas, New Delhi has remained steadfast in continuing to source petroleum from the South American country, prioritising Indian national interest, over carrying the can for other's interests. Prime Minister Modi has placed great premium on developing renewable energy as the lynchpin to sustainable development and environmental consciousness. Latin American countries have emerged as leaders and pioneers, be it a Chile which leads in solar energy production and transmission, or a Costa Rica, which has been acclaimed by the UNDP for its revolutionary compact with ecological consciousness and substantively curbing carbon footprint. The LAC region can be an arch-pillar to Prime Minister Modi's quest to globalise the International Solar Alliance, which is headquartered in India.

The Indian Prime Minister has also repeatedly spoken about cultural tourism in his signature campaigns. But these need to be aggressively highlighted. For example, the International Yoga Day was celebrated at Machu Pichu in the Peruvian Highlands, however, did not receive adequate coverage, both in the state and private media. Had this been done, Latin America would have reverberated amongst the Indian masses. Long physical distances do deter people to people exchanges in person; however, if the media fails to highlight events, then the disincentive stands compounded. Colombia, which once was synonymous with the breeding, consumption and trafficking of narcotics, alone, has today seen its towns such as Medellin, brimming with tourist footfalls, from around the world.

It is also not well known that India's flagship Mahatma Gandhi National Rural Employment Guarantee Act, 2005 (MGNREGA), has a Latin America connect. In 2005, the then ruling Congress party sent a delegation to Brazil, under the chairmanship of then Delhi Chief Minister Sheila Dikshit to study the Brazilian direct benefit transfer program called 'Bolsa Familia.' This was a very powerful financial and social inclusion measure, enacted by President Lula during his two term tenure in office (2002-2010), that led to a significant lowering of school dropout rate, and in 2005, the United Nations declared it to be a pioneering program, in the developing world. This, in many ways became the lead for MGNREGA. Co-operation between India and the LAC countries hence can be mutually beneficial. India has much to learn and much to give too, especially in offering technological innovations which are frugal and also pioneering in the field of financial and social inclusion.

When India looks at Latin America, it must also look into how China operates and cultivates a region, even if they do so for their vested interests. Prime Minister Manmohan Singh went to Brazil for BRICS Summit in 2005 and 2009 and to Mexico in 2012 for the G20. And Prime Minister Modi went to Brazil for BRICS Summit in 2014, to Mexico for a four hour stop-over, quintessentially on a NSG canvassing swing in 2016, and to Buenos Aires, for the G20 in 2018. What is conspicuous is that there is no visible Prime Ministerial visit to the region. As against this, the Chinese President has gone thrice to Latin America, in his first five-year term, each time visiting at least three countries, covering nine countries in all. Premier Li Keqiang visits every alternate year and the head of NPC (National People's Congress), has also been to the region. They have divided countries among themselves. India is also trying to do this through visits by the President and Vice President, but we know how powerful the Prime Minister's visit can be in comparison. Prime Minister Modi is adept in breaking the moulds in foreign policy and also the hiatus in foreign policy. He was the first PM to visit Australia in 28 years, the UAE in 34 years, and one hopes he will the first Prime Minister to visit the region of Latin America in 50 years.

# 30

## India-Russia Relations

*P.S. Raghavan*

India-Russia relations is an integral part of India's Foreign Policy and is a perfect example of multi-aligned policy. It's a development of India's International Relations (IR) with multiple power nations for mutual benefit. Recently, 70 years of the India-Russia relationship were celebrated, but the relationship is much more than that.

Immediately after independence, Russia (the then Soviet Union) supported India's development the most. Steel plants, be it at Bokaro or at Bhilai, were built with Soviet assistance. The Soviet Union also supported India in other industries like pharmaceuticals, electrical, etc., at a time when the Indian economy was an agrarian one. India also received political support, especially in the dispute with Pakistan over J&K, when international support was required to preserve India's security. The Soviet Union used their veto powers on two important occasions in the UNSC, without which India may not have been what it is today. These enabled India to free Goa from Portuguese rule and make it a part of India. During the Bangladesh Liberation War in 1971, the Soviet Union once again used its veto power in favour of India which enabled the war to end on Indian terms and led to the creation of Bangladesh. The role played by the Soviet Union in strengthening India's defence and military preparedness, also helped India during both the 1965 and 1971 wars with Pakistan.

Altruism as a concept does not exist in IR. During the Cold War, there were two blocs, the Western Bloc (The United States, its NATO allies and others) and the Eastern Bloc (the Soviet Union and its allies in the Warsaw Pact), both driving their geopolitical agendas. Pakistan joined the Western

Bloc led by the US and later facilitated the US outreach to China. Both the US and China supported Pakistan in the 1965 War as well as in the Liberation War of 1971 and the USSR came out in India's support. India, at that time was a part of the Non-Aligned Movement (NAM), trying to maintain an equidistance from the two power blocs. But what people have usually not projected is NAM as being an autonomous power of developing nations to channelise their interest through these power blocs—the US and USSR—and that is the India-USSR link.

The Cold War ended with the break up of the Soviet Union. Now China is emerging as a new power bloc and with that, the world scenario is once again witnessing change. New challenges are now creating new opportunities and avenues to increase ones network. Therefore, this is being tapped by all nations and it is in this context that we need to understand India-Russia relations today. IR is never based on nostalgia or gratitude but on current and future relevance. So we need to evaluate India-Russia relations through these parameters. Today, India is a strong nation, both politically and economically. It has strong relations with US, EU and Japan. On the other hand, Russia is no longer a super power. In fact after 2014, they had a stand-off with the West and there is this narrative that it has become weak after constant pressure from the West. But Russia now has strong relations with China. Another factor is the Pakistan angle, with Russia now supplying arms to Pakistan. When we look at these canvases, it is relevant to ask whether India should seek a partner in Russia. Is Russia still important? Is it strong enough to support India, as it had done in the past and are Russian geopolitical aspirations conducive to support relations with India as in yesteryears?

Let us examine the first question and look into the present range of India-Russia cooperation. Since 2000, onwards, a new phase in the relationship started, after Putin became the President. India's reliance on Russia has however not decreased because India still holds 60-70 per cent of its arms which are of Soviet/Russian origin, and these need constant repair and maintenance. If we look at the statistics from 2012-16, 68 per cent of Indian arms came from Russia and only 14 per cent from the US. So India still has great reliance on Russia as it is not able to get similar kind of technological advanced weapon systems from other countries. The very recent S 400 Air Defence System, being procured by India from Russia is considered as a state of the art system—a fact even accepted by NATO. India's nuclear submarines have also come from Russia. Hence, the India-Russia defence relationship has not been replaced by any other relationship.

Nuclear energy is another sector. Russia is the only country which develops nuclear energy in India. In 2008, the NSG led by the US accorded a waiver for India which opened the doors for civil nuclear cooperation with India. However, India's civil liability legislation has prevented most countries from coming to India, and so far, it is Russia which is extending support. Russia also supports supply and lifecycle maintenance of these nuclear plants. Two plants are already functional and a couple more are in the pipeline with a commitment of 30,000 MW of nuclear power generation in India.

With respect to hydrocarbons, Russia has invested in India's oil and gas industry, with a USD 13 billion investment when they bought 98 per cent of Essar's ports and refinery in Gujarat. In Eurasian Economic Union, India is negotiating a Free Trade Agreement (FTA). There is also a north-south transport corridor that India is seeking to make with Russia and Iraq which will go from India to Iraq and thence to Russia and into North Europe. This is both an economic as well as strategic move, that will cut the distance between India and North Europe by half.

Is Russia still important? Russia to a large extent has survived to sustain itself through the isolation. IMF says Russia is growing economically and it has played an important role in the global situation around Iraq, North Korea, Syria, including the nuclear deal and taking out a large amount of Uranium from Iran. In effect, Russia has manoeuvred itself to regain importance in the political power play in the world. It remains a permanent UNSC member and all these factors put together make Russia an important part of global affairs.

With respect to the last question, India and Russia have taken part in a number of events and the Annual India-Russia summit still continues to showcase the relationship commitment of both the countries. Russia itself looks at India as an important link in surviving in the multipolar world today. Even while it is strengthening its relation with China, it seeks to maintain its relation with Vietnam and Japan as a counterbalance. So, all evidence points to the fact that Russia is interested in maintaining strong relations with India. The world has changed, and India does not have an exclusive relationship with Russia. Just as India has moved ahead and forged relationships with other countries, so has Russia, which has also strengthened its relations with other

South Asian countries. This is a balancing effort which does not impinge on the importance of the India-Russia relationship to both countries.

In conclusion, defence remains a vital component of India's relations with Russia. India will try to diversify its military acquisitions to get the best technology available, but even in this, Russian leverage can be used. Great power relations are not a zero-sum game. So, we need not cut ties with Russia to maintain ties with the US, Europe and other countries. India is focussed on bilateral relations with other countries and the fact that it is friendly with one has no bearing on its friendship with another as each relationship is important. As an example, The India-US relationship is important to drive the Indo-Pacific agenda as a response to China and we need to preserve these relations. Russia is also our neighbours neighbour, so India needs to maintain power to influence power play in the neighbourhood. And finally, Russia is investing in India in economic terms.

India needs to sustain the strategic partnership with Russia and broaden the relationship, looking beyond defence and moving into other sectors like oil and gas, education and science to ensure vibrancy. In todays geographical power play, as India navigates through these bilateral partnerships, it needs to diversify and strengthen these relations.

# 31

## India and the United Kingdom

*Rahul Roy-Chaudhury*

I have been living and working in the UK for nearly 15 years now and in the past few years have witnessed an amazing transformation of the 'power dynamics' of the India-UK relationship—whereas earlier the UK was more important to India than India was to the UK, today, the reverse is true, that is India has become more important to the UK than the UK is to India. Essentially, this means that it is now Britain that is keener to engage with India than the other way round, giving rise to a relatively advantageous political position for India. Four reasons come to mind, why I believe this to be so.

First, India is currently the fastest-growing large economy in the world—growing even faster than China—and the seventh largest economy in the world. With projected growth rates, including of the just-released Economic Survey, of 7.5 per cent growth in 2018-19, India's economy is set to overtake the UK as the fifth largest global economy by end 2018, early 2019. Indeed, as this year's IISS Military Balance indicates, India has, for the first time, overtaken the UK in defence spending. India has the fifth largest defence budget in the world, at USD 52.5 billion in 2017, exceeding the UK's defence budget of USD 50.7 billion in 2017.

Second, India is the third largest foreign investor in the UK with more investments in the UK than the rest of the EU. An Indian company, TATA, is the second largest employer in the UK, employing over 110,000 people; and approximately 800 Indian-owned companies currently operate in the UK today.

Third, India's growing economy has provided—under Prime Minister Narendra Modi—an energetic, vibrant, bold and innovative foreign policy that seeks to transform India from a 'balancing' to a 'leading' global and regional power. This has led to an extraordinary level of bilateral engagements with India—all you need to do is chart the number of foreign leaders visiting India in the last three years compared to earlier and you will see my point.

Fourth, as a result of this, the UK is now one among several countries actively seeking to engage with India. The UK is also now only India's 17th largest trading partner (in 2016-17), with USD 12.2 billion in bilateral trade, amounting to less than two per cent of India's overall trade. This has fallen from the previous year. Meanwhile, Germany is India's largest trading partner in the EU, and sixth overall, with bilateral trade at USD 18.8 billion in 2016-17. I have argued elsewhere that this also means the UK is now, no longer, one of India's top 5 strategic partners.

But, this does not in any way mean that the UK is a relatively 'declining power' versus India as a 'rising power'. The UK is still important to India for four reasons:

> First, the UK is still the fifth largest economy in the world, and will remain in the top ten for some time. Second, the UK is the largest G20 investor in India (and the fourth largest investor in India after Mauritius, Singapore and Japan) with a cumulative equity investment of nearly USD 25 billion (April 2000-June 2017). In effect, the UK accounted for around 7 per cent of all FDI into India for the period April 2000–June 2017. In 2016–17, UK FDI to India was USD 1.2 billion, an increase of USD 300 million from the previous year. Third, London is the leading global financial centre, where in August 2016, the world's first ever "masala" or rupee-denominated bond issued outside of India was listed on the London Stock Exchange. Fourth, the UK is a nuclear weapon state and Permanent Member of the UN Security Council, and also wields considerable influence through its comprehensive and enviable network of regional and global strategic partnerships.

It was for these reasons that Prime Minister Narendra Modi's visit to the UK in November 2015 attempted to provide momentum to a bilateral relationship that felt tired and sluggish, with both countries all too familiar with each other.

## The UK and Brexit

The past 18 months have also been the most significant in terms of 'political disruption' in the UK's relationship with the EU in over four decades, through the prospective British exit from the EU (called Brexit), which has implications for India—both short-term and medium term. Within seven months of Prime Minister Narendra Modi's November 2015 visit to Britain, the British people voted to leave the EU. But, the result of the British referendum on this issue was very close—with those wanting to leave the EU winning the vote by 51.9 per cent to 48.1 per cent. Whereas, England (although not London) and Wales voted for Brexit, Scotland and Northern Ireland both backed staying in the EU.

This immediately resulted in domestic political turmoil and confusion over the EU, both of which continue to persist today. British Prime Minister David Cameron immediately resigned; Theresa May, the then Home Secretary (Minister) became the new Prime Minister without facing a full Conservative leadership contest; and then, surprisingly, she called a snap general election on 8 June 2017 (which had only been due in 2020) which she went on to win but with fewer seats, and therefore had to form a weaker minority government (with the support of the 10 MPs from Northern Ireland's Democratic Unionist Party). This has resulted in deep divisions within her Cabinet between Brexiteers and 'Remainers' as well as challenges to her own leadership.

Added to this, is the prevailing confusion over what British Prime Minister May actually meant when she said that 'Brexit means Brexit.' For, there is no clear indication of what she actually wants or what the other 27 EU states are prepared to give her. With May invoking Article 50 of the Treaty of Lisbon on 29 March 2017, she now has till 29 March 2019 to agree to the terms of the split. This includes the rights of British and EU expatriate citizens after Brexit; reaching a figure for the amount of money Britain will need to pay on leaving the EU, which is known as the 'divorce bill'; and what happens to the border between Northern Ireland (which as part of the UK will be leaving the EU), and the Republic of Ireland (which remains in the EU). There is also expected to be an 18-24 months implementation/transition period from 29 March 2019.

There appear to be three basic scenarios:

First, a 'Hard Brexit,' involving the UK leaving the EU Single Market (which allows the free movement of goods, services, money and people within the EU as if it were a single country) and the Customs Union (which allows member states to trade freely with each other, without burdensome customs checks at borders, but it limits their freedom to strike their own trade deals).

Second, a 'Soft Brexit,' involving Britain remaining within the Customs Union, but likely with the EU insisting that it accepts the free movement of people, goods, capital and services.

Third, 'No Brexit deal.' May has said she would rather take Britain out of the EU with "no deal" rather than a 'bad deal.' Without an agreement on trade, Britain would have to operate under World Trade Organisation (WTO) rules, which could mean customs checks and tariffs on goods as well as longer border checks for travellers.

Whatever the final result, the UK government's own analysts have stated that the UK will be 'worse off' in every scenario of Brexit.

## Impact of Changed Bilateral Dynamics and Brexit

And, Finally, what is the impact of the greater importance of India for the UK and Brexit on the future bilateral relationship between the UK and India? What we do know, is that the whole issue of Brexit has proved to be a setback of four plus years for the planned transformation of bilateral relations between the UK and India. The reason is that since June 2016, the UK has been overwhelmingly consumed politically over the issue of Brexit and the future relationship with the EU. I have often said that the UK currently has three foreign policy priorities—Brexit, Brexit and Brexit! With India's general elections within the next 18 months, this effectively means that both sides will have to lower their sights on bilateral ambitions for at least the next three years, till mid-2021.

But, in terms of the short-term bilateral relationship, we simply do not know what the future holds in terms of trade and investment ties, as it will depend on what sort of Brexit finally takes place—'hard,' 'soft' or 'no deal.' However, because of Brexit, in the medium term, there could be a new India-UK Free Trade Agreement (FTA) to maintain existing bilateral trade. But any negotiation of such a trade agreement can only take place after the completion of the UK's negotiation with the EU in March 2019, and only implemented after the transition phase which will be another 18–24 months. Therefore, an India-UK FTA will most likely not be implemented until 2021 at the earliest.

The potential benefits of an India-UK FTA have, however, been questioned as the UK only accounted for 3 per cent of total Indian exports in 2016–17. One should also bear in mind that the India-EU FTA has not succeeded, in significant part, because the UK had opposed it. Therefore, India-UK discussions on FTA are likely be difficult. In this context, India and the UK have already set up trade committees to discuss an FTA, including the India-UK Joint Economic & Trade Committee (JETCO) (the 12th JETCO meeting was held in London on 11 January 2018 between Commerce Minister Suresh Prabhu and UK International Trade Secretary Dr. Liam Fox); the Finance Ministerial-led Economic and Financial Dialogue (9th meeting was held in Delhi in April 2017); and the financial services-led Financial Partnership. Therefore, in the Medium Term, Brexit could provide key opportunities for both the India-UK broader political as well as the narrower trade and investment relationships.

In this endeavour, there is a clear outreach from the UK to India. The UK government has rhetorically stated its approach of 'a global Britain' and 'continuing to be an outward looking nation.' It has also emphasised that economic and trade relations with India will be a top priority. Significantly, India was the destination of British Prime Minister May's first major bilateral visit outside the EU in November 2016. And, in terms of the changed power dynamics in the India-Britain relationship, India can be expected take a hard bargaining position over trade access versus greater liberalisation of the British visa regime and overcoming visa hurdles for Indian students and for intra-company transfers, for movement of professionals.

As the Indian economy prepares to overtake the UK as the world's fifth largest economy, one thing is clear: that the 'power dynamics' of the traditional India-UK relationship have dramatically changed with, for the first time, India more important to the UK than the UK is to India, and that the success of a post-Brexit India-UK FTA is expected to reflect this new reality.

# 32

## India and the European Union

*Ranjan Mathai*

The EU encompasses most of Europe today, so it is useful to begin with a brief look at the historical background of the relations between these two subcontinents.

India and Europe are geopolitically, sub-continental regions at two ends of the Eurasian landmass. Despite distance, they have been historically linked by migration, trade, culture and even conquest. After all, Alexander's quest for world conquest reached its limits in India. Indians traded with Rome in a later era, and there are famous complaints by Roman writers about their trade deficit with India! Trade was both overland and by the maritime routes chronicled in the Periplus of the Erythrean Sea. In more recent times, India's reputation as the land of great riches, made it loom large in European imagination and brought traders, adventurers and conquerors to our territory.

When the era of colonialism came to an end, India and Europe were substantial trading partners. Independent India took great interest in Europe, even though it was emerging from the devastation of WW II; and we viewed its nations as major actors in global affairs. This trend continued as the European Economic Community which emerged between the 1950s and 1970s, acquired a vast network of trade and influence worldwide. India established formal ties with the EEC in 1962 (Note that this was when Britain was not in the community), being one of the first "developing" countries to do so.

Relations developed substantially and the EEC became a major trading, investment, and later a development partner for India—a source of financial and technical assistance. The cooperation agreements of 1973 (again India was the first foreign partner to reach this kind of agreement with the EEC) and later in 1981, gave legal form to these steadily expanding ties. Both the investment and trade relations did not grow as fast as those of EEC with some other partners, largely because of India's somewhat autarchic policies and failure to craft investment friendly policies. But throughout the last 55 years since relations were established, the EEC (now EU) has been a major, if not the major trading partner for India.

The EEC became the EU following the Maastricht Treaty of 1992 just as the Cold War ended and the reunification of Germany took place; I was in Brussels in 1991–93 when the transformation took place, and recall the great interest with which India followed the setting of the Union—a possible independent pole in world affairs. It had three pillars, and we followed the development of all: the European Community mostly for trade and investment; the Common Foreign & Security Policy—to coordinate foreign policies; and, to a lesser extent, the home/judicial pillar. India engaged closely and regularly with the newly empowered European Parliament and built inter-parliamentary relations. By 1993, India completed a Joint Political Statement to develop institutionalised political dialogue between the EU Troika and India and regular exchanges over CFSP. In 1994, India moved to a 3rd Generation Cooperation Agreement which upgraded India's overall relationship .

Some EU leaders announced the "hour of Europe" as having arrived in the early 1990s. The hour did not come—as seen by failure to tackle the fallout of the breakup of Yugoslavia. Later, the EU expanded from 12 to 27 members and, as some anticipated, its external actions became even less unified and independent. The EU reliance on NATO for security, for example, did not decrease. However, India went forward in building political ties, and some years later a scheme of Annual Summits between Indian and EU leaders was put in place, starting in Lisbon in 2000. The high level exchanges led to a Strategic Partnership in 2004. An agenda of actions under this partnership was drawn up in the Joint Action Plan of 2005, which was reviewed in 2008.

The decade after the first Summit in 2000 saw trade volumes more than doubling. Based on the Strategic Partnership, the relationship grew substantively, taking into account the new global dynamics, and the emergence of India and the EU as bigger players in global affairs. A number of sectoral dialogue mechanisms were initiated, on energy, space, education, S&T, maritime and civil aviation transport, and from 2006, on security (Counter-terrorism, counter-piracy, and cyber security). An ambitious plan for a Broad-based Trade and Investment Agreement (BTIA), often called FTA was launched in 2007.

There has, however, been a hiatus between 2012–15 when strains emerged in ties between India and some EU countries as well as with the EU. The economic crisis of 2007–8 and its aftermath left the EU struggling to cope with the "Eurozone crisis" as well as with protectionist impulses, and the growth of anti-EU sentiment in Britain and some other member states. These problems were exacerbated by discords over issues like the arrest of Italian naval personnel involved in the killing of Indian fishermen. The BTIA negotiations got stuck on both substance and a lack of political will. It was only in 2016, when the 13th Summit was held after a gap of four years that some momentum has been restored. Those four years were a difficult time; Some joked that the attitudes varied on both sides on the lines of the old joke between Austrians and Germans:

*G: Situation is serious but not hopeless.*

*A: Situation is hopeless but not serious!*

But on a more serious note, let us look at some facts and figures today. These are reflected in the outcome of the last (14th) Indo-EU Summit in Delhi in October 2017. The EU is still India's largest trading partner (13 per cent of India's trade), China being second at 11 per cent. When you look at exports, EU takes almost 17 per cent of India's exports while China takes less than 5 per cent! For the EU, India is the 9th largest trade partner. The EU, collectively, is the second largest source of FDI into India after Mauritius. For India's FDI, the EU is the number one destination (UK is the largest within EU).

## Strategic Partnership in Foreign and Security Affairs

The India-EU Joint Statement declares that, as the world's largest democracies, with shared values of freedom, equality, tolerance, and rule of law, we are partners in upholding a rules-based international order; with respect for international law and norms; working for peace and stability in an interconnected and multipolar world. A Joint Declaration was issued on counter-terrorism, cooperation in tackling foreign terrorists, terrorist financing and arms supply. This specifically identifies individuals and groups based in Pakistan.

India has dialogues on regional affairs of vital concern to both (Afghanistan, Bangladesh-Myanmar, Iran, DPRK, Syria, MEPP, ASEM, Ukraine, Africa), disarmament, counter-terrorism, on migration, refugees, and on climate change. In regard to climate actions, it is noteworthy that the European Investment Bank will invest Euro 800 million in India on climate action/renewable energy projects. It will also fund solar energy development in other solar rich countries, in keeping with the aims of the International Solar Alliance initiated by the Prime Minister of India.

India is also committed to safeguarding global commons—sea lanes, cyberspace and outer space. In the Indian Ocean, the respective navies cooperate on counter-piracy and other maritime security operations. The EU Naval Force participated in joint exercises with the Indian Navy (IN) in PASSEX (A Passage exercise done between two navies to ensure that the navies are able to communicate and cooperate in times of war or humanitarian relief), off the coast of Somalia (Interestingly, an Italian flagship led the EU Naval Force, suggesting that the era of bad ties with Italy is behind us!). Both India and the EU support UNCLOS and want to develop a blue economy. India's oceanographic research teams have also cooperated with teams from Germany and other countries in the past.

It was agreed to enhance space cooperation, including earth observation. India has a rich history of cooperation with France, and this was expanded in the 1980s when ISRO began cooperation with the European Space Agency (established in 1973) for launch of educational/communication satellites and meteorological applications. Both sides also agreed to push an agreement on civil nuclear cooperation between European Atomic Energy Community (EAEC or Euratom) and India's Department of Atomic Energy (DAE). Cooperation with France and other countries on nuclear energy already exists but the EU level agreement will introduce a higher level of certainty for the future. Presently, India and the EU are also partners (out of six worldwide) in the International Thermonuclear Energy Research Project in France.

## Sectoral Cooperation in Research and Innovation

This is a sector of cooperation with the EU that is, and will continue to be, of great significance for India (Particularly for young people, far removed from the arenas of government engagements). India is already one of the largest beneficiaries of the EU's Erasmus education initiative, and the Summit welcomed the fact that there are now over 5000 Indian alumni. There will be enhanced cooperation on energy and climate change, competition policy, urban development and migration. These policy dialogues are significant for India's enhanced integration into the global economic framework. In earlier times, Indian regulations for anti-dumping and even single-market rules benefited from EU experience. Transport is another sector in which the two sides are expanding cooperation. The Indo-EU Horizontal Agreement on Air Services is to be operationalised, which will give firm legal basis for the expanded EU airlines operations in India. The EIB agreed to provide financing for the Bangalore Metro, which will be appreciated by the harassed travellers of that city, just as much as the Delhiites are of the Japanese funding of Delhi Metro!

## Culture and Policy

I believe to understand why the potential for cooperation between India and the EU is as great as I believe it is, it is necessary to view the cultural underpinning of the relationship. India has had long standing cultural ties with the people of Europe. Today, being linked through the Indo-European group of languages, makes both culturally more intelligible to each other, especially as there is widespread use of English in both our territories. Both believe in unity in diversity and both are committed to secularism in government, even as both have a single dominant religion. Both the polities are strongly affected by the upsurge of identity politics and the efforts to introduce religious tones into national discourse, both in our own domestic affairs and in the external arenas. For both India and the EU, the turbulence within the world of Islam is simultaneously a domestic issue, and a challenge on their respective borders. The Founding Principles of both emerged from a post WWII political and economic order. And both face centripetal forces of diversity, challenging common purposes as well as antediluvian notions challenging the secular basis of their political orders. It is often forgotten that the constitutional ideals of both were enunciated and accepted, to avert the repetition of tragic developments in their histories! There is no doubt that the outcome of both our constitutional experiments, to maintain open, liberal societies will be historically significant on a global scale. That is why I would say that India and the EU are Strategic Partners.

But are we Strategic Partners? There is a definitional issue here. In business, a strategic partnership suggests a common enterprise arrangement that falls short of being a legal partnership. Similarly, in foreign affairs, a strategic partnership connotes long-term interaction, based on political, economic, social and historical factors. This manifests itself in a variety of relationships and common endeavours. While it is not a formal alliance by treaty, it connotes a very substantive relationship with capacity for joint action when needed, and agreed upon. When I left government in 2013, India had about 30 strategic partnerships, only some of which included a substantive political-military (pol-mil) dimension. The EU has only 10 strategic partners, of which four are in Asia (Japan, China, S. Korea and India). With the EU, the pol-mil dimension with India is limited, largely because the EU's military dimension is limited, but this could change.

EU officials complain that Indian policy makers do not approach the EU strategically in global affairs; the fact is that for Indian policy makers dealing with defence, homeland security, intelligence, and even nuclear energy, and space, the reality is that they have to deal with national capitals, particularly Paris, Berlin and London, rather than Brussels to get delivery of desired outcomes. In 2008, India's Prime Minister, after the India-EU Summit in Marseilles, pointedly remarked in response to media queries on India's first civil nuclear agreement (which was with France) that he would discuss the substance with the French President the next day during a bilateral interaction in Paris! It needs to be said however, that even after completion of negotiations in Paris we had to wait for Euratom endorsement before the agreement came into force.

There was a time when the trajectory of the EU was heading towards greater integration. There was talk of joint defence arrangements, and more cross-border defence manufacturing which would get EU oversight. Space cooperation considered new horizons with plans for India to work with ESA on the Galileo programme. After Brexit and challenges from Italy, Hungary etc to greater integration, the picture has become blurred. Some of our commentators believe that policy makers here have already decided that a breakup of the EU is now a real possibility. With so much invested in this project for so long, this seems unlikely at present. But it remains to be seen whether a new German-French motor can drive a new phase of integration for all the remaining 27, or in a "2 phase" EU. In particular, for the EU's relations with India to gain weight beyond the economic sphere, we would need to see whether EU's External Action Service, which coordinates EU member state delegations/missions, acquires responsibility for security, including counter-terrorism and intelligence, and whether common defence structures come under the jurisdiction of Brussels.

Analysts in Brussels sometimes compared India's approach with that of China, which in the past appeared to use its strategic partnership with EU to achieve geopolitical goals, seeking a counterpoise to US unipolarity. That phase has gone after 2008, and it now seems that China's purpose was to enlarge its economic and commercial markets, and hedge currency options at a time of US dominance, while neutralising EU's concerns over human rights and democracy.

The issue of 'human rights' brings us to a dimension which could be either a stumbling block or a bridge to enhance our relations. The EUs prescriptive/normative approach has sometimes been viewed as having little relevance to India, and often oblivious of India's concerns. Preaching to India on human rights causes irritation, especially as EU's failure to be firm in denouncing terrorism sponsored from outside against India, made Indian officials question the relevance of dialogue with the EU. Interestingly, this normative structure has been questioned in Europe itself, particularly as constant additions of conditionality's in EU programs over social, environmental, even personal behavioural norms, has introduced absurd rigidities into EU negotiating style. Timothy Garton Ash once responded to a request for a joke about EU by noting that EU norms were now so difficult, that if the EU applied for membership of EU today it would not be admitted!

That said, it is necessary to stress the importance of large, multi-cultural democracies like India and the EU to continue to be supportive of freedom, democracy, diversity, and open societies without being subjectively prescriptive. Clearly, trends towards intolerance, and restrictions on freedom in India will inhibit the development of ties with the EU. Similarly, growth of racism or xenophobia in EU will diminish the scope for cooperation with India. To invert Ash, recall the one liner of Groucho Marx who said he would not join any club which was willing to have someone like himself as a member! So, what of the future?

We now live in a different world from a year ago. Both India and the EU believe in multipolarity and balance in global affairs. Unipolarity or the Chinese vision of a G-2 would not be acceptable to either. The Chinese plans for dominance of Eurasia through the Belt and Road Initiative aroused Indian apprehensions immediately. It now appears that EU is also having second thoughts. A leading EU Parliamentarian declared that while it is OK to link Asia with Europe, it is necessary to be clear about principles. Earlier, EU member states seemed to be falling over each other to woo Chinese investments and host the launch of the international yuan. Now there are concerns over Chinese investments/loans leading to acquisition of physical assets in EU (e.g. Greece) currency manipulation, and trade practices (pressures to transfer technologies/IPRs, lack of reciprocity in opening markets etc) as well as industrial espionage.

For the EU, India's continued fast-paced growth, its large GDP, its openness to trade (India's trade intensity of GDP is today higher then EU) and its improvement in ease of doing business make it vital in a world of weak demand and low, albeit increasing, growth. If India's growth and investment rates accelerate, it could match the "China effect" on world growth of the early 2000s.

The long-term success of the Euro would be useful for India in a world of dollar dominance and unpredictability of US policies. During the financial crisis of 2007, countries such as China, Russia and Iran had moved to diversify their reserves by increasing holdings in euros; India is also believed to have diversified more into the euro, but since the RBI does not provide data on the breakup of its holdings, actual figures are hard to come by. The subsequent Euro zone crisis however halted this trend. Today, with the Chinese projecting the yuan as an alternate international currency, India needs another hedge, which could be the euro if the EU pulls together with greater financial integration. As of now the constraint is that the ECB is not as responsive and flexible as required due to the diverse agendas of member states. The US liquid pool of assets is still bigger than other markets. But SWIFT data shows that the euro remains not far behind the dollar as the currency of international payments

Both EU and India are maritime powers which have an interest in keeping sea-lanes of communication open and free from piracy or exclusivity. Eurasia is today in turmoil and the Indian Ocean–Mediterranean region are its boundaries. India has demonstrated capacity and willingness to cooperate with EU in the maritime domain. The EU would need to step up its strategic stake in India and specifically support a larger place for India in world affairs. It could start by resolving its internal cohesion to support India's Permanent membership of the UNSC, and the NSG.

It is necessary for both India and EU to show long term vision and move towards completion of a Broad-based Trade & Investment Agreement (BTIA).

This has been under negotiation since 2007–8. The last occasion it seemed nearing conclusion, it was reopened by EU demands on automobiles and wines/spirits; and India remained determined to push harder for trade in services with access for natural persons to IT markets. EU should now recognise India's moves to align with EU requirements and give India "data secure" status. India's unilateral withdrawal from BIPPAs, has not helped matters. Its current model BIT excludes matters relating to taxation, tariff reductions, and has nuanced the provisions for national treatment of foreign investors. A new Bilateral Investment Protection Treaty with the EU would build confidence and enhance investments required for the Make in India thrust of the PM. Perhaps India could resolve the impasse by new approaches to Multilateral Investment Courts to resolve disputes. These are all issues for negotiations, but it is really for the EU to show long-term vision; it is after all, the largest trading bloc which has not been able to reach a FTA with any major partner in the last decade.

The EU must also demonstrate greater political support for India's efforts to tackle the critical threats it faces. During the Doklam standoff the EU was silent, while both Japan and the US spoke out in support of India. Member state issues, based on local politics still prevents the EU from taking a clear stance on India's side in the battle against Pakistani supported terrorism directed against India. India for its part has not been able to share EU perspectives over the situation in Ukraine, as it remains close to Russia. There are therefore serious issues in the way of real parallelism of interests. But with China in assertive mode, and US policies uncertain, our geopolitical convergences and common values make us natural partners in a world of flux and change. Maritime cooperation can be extended with EU joining Japan and India in partnership to counter the Chinese drive for hegemony. France is an Indian Ocean/Pacific power so the basis does exist to set up a cooperative framework

## Brexit

It is necessary to say a few words on Brexit. Clearly, India has very great interests in both UK and EU and hopes the negotiations conclude in a way that imposes least obstacles for continued growth in our ties with both sides. A hard Brexit could impact the future of 800 plus Indian companies in the UK. The UK takes 20 per cent of India's overall exports to the EU, but as much as 50 per cent of our IT services export to the EU. Britain has been a supporter for India on many issues in EU counsels; conversely, the British concern over expanding its market for spirits in India has been a sticking point in the BTIA negotiations.

Brexit will not alter the maritime outlook of the EU , though there will be incentives for Europe to cooperate more on Eurasian land links with China and Central Asia. On areas of sectoral cooperation, the EU will continue to be a valued partner; though the use of English language is now taken for granted when making this assumption. It is time for renewed determination in both Delhi and Brussels to build a stronger Strategic Partnership. India could respond to the vigour demonstrated by President Macron and Chancellor Merkel to make the EU an independent pole in world affairs. The EU must deal with India as an Indo-Pacific power, and demonstrate that it views the Rise of India as being in its own interest.

# 33

# India-Africa Relations

*Virendra Gupta*

India's relationship with Africa is a subject of considerable importance both emotionally and in material terms. This is the region which is geographically closer to India, although I would not say that it is a part of our neighbourhood. We have a historical connect with this region and some writings would suggest that the contacts existed from the time of the Indus Valley civilisation in India. There had been extensive trading links between the western coast of India and the eastern sea ports of Africa. Many traders from India routinely made trips on the sail boats, taking advantage of the favourable sea breeze, and set up their bases in the eastern sea ports such as Mombasa and Zanzibar.

India-Africa relations are characterised by extensive people-to-people contacts which have existed for the last several centuries. One of the most notable aspect of this is the presence of a strong Indian diaspora in Africa. There are about 3 million people of Indian origin spread across Africa and they are contributing a great deal towards the socio-economic development of their adopted countries. Many of them are participating in politics as well. There might have been some resentment against them earlier because of their visible presence in retail trade, but in the present times there is a wide appreciation for their hard work and contribution made by them to the economic development of their respective countries. The values espoused by them and their sincerity has earned them admiration and respect all around.

I am mentioning it because this year (2018) we are commemorating the centenary of the formal end of the indentureship practice. It was introduced around 1838 after abolition of slavery to beat the labour shortages in sugarcane and cocoa plantations in the British colonial territories. A lot of people were taken out of India to these far off places and subjected to very difficult, oppressive and inhuman conditions. They hung on to whatever was in store for them, only to provide a better life for their children. They maintained deep emotional attachment to the country of their origin and the cultural values that they had brought with them from India. We need to actually have a sense of gratitude to these people, who stood by the Indian values and for having accomplished complete transformation of their socio-economic condition. They have made India proud.

The vibrant and well diversified economic cooperation constitutes an important pillar of the India–Africa relationship. The bilateral trade stands at about USD 70 billion, and India's investments in Africa total around USD 55 billion. The investments are spread across key sectors. Africa is one of the fastest growing regions of the world which has sustained a high level of economic growth for the last several years. The mineral resources in Africa have drawn worldwide interest and you are aware of aggressive policies followed by China in acquiring these resources. India's interest in the mineral resources available in Africa has also grown over the years and we have now begun to source fairly significant portions of our crude oil as well as coal requirements from Africa. In that sense, Africa has helped India meet its critical energy security needs by way of diversification of energy resources which is extremely important.

While these economic bonds and linkages have grown over the years serviced by extensive and multi-layered political contacts, the relationship between India and Africa cannot be measured in economic terms alone. In fact, I would regard that as a relatively smaller part of our relationship matrix. The more important aspect is the shared past of colonial subjugation and suffering. This cannot be dismissed merely as a rhetorical assertion. It actually plays out a lot in the African psyche.

I would describe India's relationship with Africa as one between brothers which engenders a sense of equality and that is what makes the India–Africa relationship very unique. This relationship can be leveraged but there is also a danger that we can inadvertently hurt the sensitivities of African countries thereby damaging the relationship. In my opinion, India has to take extreme care in avoiding the latter pitfall. When Africans see the models of development in China or for that matter in Europe and America, they admire it, but perhaps do not relate to it in the way they relate to the model of development in India as something they can aspire to replicate in their own countries. This feeling of oneness that the Africans share with India is the most distinguishing feature of our relationship.

India's investments in Africa have grown consistently. In the third India–Africa forum summit, India announced large amount of new soft credit lines, and considerable funds were also set aside as outright grant. All of that will seek to supplement India's fairly substantial economic assistance programme to Africa. Having said that, I must reiterate that our relationship with Africa cannot and should not be benchmarked to the quantum of money that India is able to provide to African countries. There is a mistaken belief in some quarters including in the government, both in the previous dispensation and probably to some extent in the present government as well since habits and perceptions die hard, that we should earmark more and more funds for Africa to drive the relationship forward. If India were to set out such benchmarks, it would be very difficult for us to compete with China which can bring far greater amounts of cash on the table, and so can the EU, Japan and the US. India should actually be leveraging its strengths in other areas for the mutual advantage of both Africa and India.

India's strength is in terms of its capacity to contribute to human resources and skill development and I think African countries have a lot of expectation from India in that field. In my interaction with the African people and African leadership during my several assignments in Africa, I realised that African countries were really not looking for cash assistance from India which they can easily get from somewhere else. They would much rather have India provide assistance that would contribute to their development aspirations. In fact, several African leaders at the highest level told me of a common saying in Africa "do not give us fish, teach us how to fish". As such, providing assistance in terms of food grains supply might be good, as it would help in addressing food security issues but it would be far better to help them achieve higher agricultural productivity for self sufficiency in food production. India's experience in the agricultural sector would be extremely relevant in the African context and so would be India's experience in the small and medium enterprises sector. It may not be the most efficient manner of employment of capital and human resources, but it contributes immensely to job creation and leads to inclusive development.

The problems of developing countries being similar, India's experience is extremely relevant to the people of Africa. I think this is what the African countries are looking for in the relationship. They are appreciative of India's accomplishments and the contribution being made by India in Africa's development particularly in the areas of education and health. I once took my daughter for a medical consultation with a highly reputed professor of ENT at the medical college in Tanzania. When I asked to pay his fees, he refused to accept it and told me that he owed his medical education to India and the last thing that he would do was to take fees from an Indian Ambassador! So there are people there, who are really appreciative of what India has done and that is the route that India must continue to pursue.

India provides soft lines of credit to developing countries and a fairly significant portion of that is earmarked for Africa. At the last India-Africa Forum Summit, India decided to substantially enhance the allocation for that. Earlier, in the soft-line credits to Africa and other countries, there were reports of considerable mismanagement. There were just a handful of Indian companies to whom these projects were allotted, and once allotted, these companies, having no domain experience, would outsource the project execution. Basically, their role was that of arrangers!

When I dealt with this issue in the Ministry of External Affairs, I undertook a detailed review of the procedures with a view to streamlining the process, involving both the initial allocation of a Line of Credit and its execution. This exercise was fully supported by then Foreign Minister Pranab Mukherjee. I believe it is a work in progress. The MEA is now beginning to get more closely involved in the review and monitoring of the projects, and greater transparency as well as professionalism has been introduced. With the reforms and the streamlining that the Govt. of India has set in motion, my belief is that the delivery of Indian assistance through the soft-lines would get more efficient and we would be able to implement the identified assistance projects much faster.

With three editions of India-Africa Forum Summit having taken place, we have managed to develop some institutional mechanisms for implementing our cooperation projects at pan-African level but there have been reports of inefficiencies and delays in the delivery of our assistance. The African Union has its own limitations and over-reliance on that ought to be avoided. We would also do well to remind ourselves that the African continent is not as homogeneous as we somehow tend to believe. Therefore, it would be prudent to continue with the bilateral and regional mechanisms that India has already developed over last several decades. Africa has very strong dynamics at the regional level and in fact each region is dominated by a regional satrap. India should, therefore, continue to evolve and develop separate cooperative mechanisms with different regions.

# 34

## A German Perspective

*Martin Ney*

In every country, the fundamental role of foreign policy is to serve national interests. In India the national interests are development, growth and its aspirations to become a global player. In Germany it is wealth, retaining economic well-being and an open society among others. The fascinating aspect of our bilateral relations is that there is no contradiction on interests in pursing foreign policy. Prime Minister Modi when he visited Berlin in the end of May 2017 said that Germany and India are made for each other. Why is it so?

From the German perspective, our welfare depends on international free trade. This is why we are so grateful that the Prime Minister made such a strong pitch for free trade in Davos. We have little natural resources and we must import them. Our domestic market is comparatively small, and therefore we must export our products.

From India's perspective, to develop fast by inclusive economic growth and also in order to narrow the gap between India and China, India's economy needs more integration with the international markets. At present, India's economy largely depends on the domestic market but to become a more international player it will have to look beyond the domestic market. India therefore also depends on free trade. India also needs to attract Foreign Direct Investments.

Both Germany and India benefit from international free trade. There are five conclusions we can draw from this. First, it explains why Germany is India's sixth largest trading partner, why the EU is India's largest trading and investment partner, and is likely to remain the largest trading partner after Brexit. Second, India and Germany sit in the same boat when it comes to defending free trade. We have to defend it jointly against voices from the countries on the eastern side of the United States. Third, there is still ample room for improvement. The volume of German trade with China is ten times more than its trade with India, and we want to balance this in the future. Fourth, and most importantly, it explains why Germany wants India's success. This is why we are India's second largest bilateral donor in economic development cooperation. From our perspective, India is our largest recipient of economic development cooperation funds. Fifth, we both need to restart negotiations on an EU-India Free Trade Agreement including investment protection. Such an FTA is not just about tariffs and regulations but is about shaking globalisation—setting precedents that others may follow.

In another reason why Germany has an interest in India becoming successful and in becoming a global player is security. We all, including think tanks, need to sit down and do a sober countries to identify countries in the world with which we share fundamental principals—rule of law, free speech, forward society. When you think about it, the number of these countries around the world are limited. The other aspect is to look for countries with which we share fundamentals regarding international borders being rule based. When we look at the number of countries who believe in and implement it, the numbers are again, limited.

It is important to do this analysis because in the long run, you can join with only such countries to stabilise international borders or the insecurity in Europe or Asia. India is such a partner for us as we consider it as a net provider of stability in Asia. Further, there are huge challenges to maintaining security and stability in not only Europe but Asia too. The elephant in the room is obviously China—how do we all deal with a more assertive China? India's Foreign Secretary recently described the Belt and Road Initiative by saying that. "Trade: is the process demand oriented, is the process consultative, is the process fair including free competition, is the process compatible with existing international frameworks and does the process respect sovereignty of that country?" Whenever a country tries to set rules unilaterally it is short sighted for two reasons. First, the country may not always be in the same position of power. Second, there are always instances when a country will need the support of the international community or smaller nations.

The bottom line is whether the rules-based international order is respected. Here, Germany and India are on the same page as we both believe in respecting the rules-based international order. Unfortunately, we have a challenge in the South China Sea. Our joint support for UNCLOS and the Laws of the Seas is most important in this respect. Here, Indian, German and European interests do converge especially with respect to the Indian Ocean. The Indian Ocean today, see more than 60 per cent of the world trade passing through its waters. Germany has the second largest shipping fleet in the world. India and Germany cannot afford to be negligent of the governance of such important waters. India, Germany and the EU are committed to the idea of multilateral security in the Indian Ocean in three aspects. Firstly, we are jointly engaged in anti-piracy engagements. Secondly, Germany is also supporting the emergence of the regional framework for managing the Indian Ocean. IORA is an emerging international forum in this regard and Germany finances its secretary. Thirdly, another area of cooperation in the Indian ocean is maritime domain awareness.

There are many other areas of Indo-German relations where we already cooperate such as fighting terrorism, stabilising Afghanistan, reform of the functioning of the UN including the UN Security Council and supporting India's membership in the Nuclear Suppliers Group. I focused on the economy and security as these are areas where German, European and Indian interests converge on policy.

# 35

# The Multi-Lateral System

*Hardeep Singh Puri*

My personal reflections of India in the multilateral system, have led me to three propositions, which I wish to share. These could also be described as self-evident truisms.

The first proposition is that the multilateral system, as we know of it today, is essentially anchored in the UN, the World Bank, the IMF and the General Agreement on Tariff and Trade (GATT) which later turned into the WTO. The architecture of these organisations reflects the pre-occupations of those who designed the system in the mid-1940s when World War II was still raging. They tried to work out an architecture and design for the world, which became the post-World War II international order. The second proposition, since India was still a colony when the post-world war architecture was being worked out in 1945, it had very limited participation in the design of that architecture. The government of that day was represented but it was more in the nature of a performa representation. Our representatives did not have much of an understanding about how the post-colonial India was going to shape. The third proposition, over the years, Indian decision makers have tended to allow their personal views and preferences to be the driving force in the recommendations they have made in terms of India's interaction with the outside world.

This has not always worked to India's advantage. Most of the time, it has had negative consequences. I think this will continue to be the case unless the formulation of foreign policy is taken outside the confines of rigid governmental structures and is enlarged to get inputs from think-tanks and the outside world to include retired and practicing foreign policy professionals.

I have three examples to quote for ease of reference. One, the decision taken by Mr Nehru when, as India's Prime Minister, he took the Kashmir issue to the UN. I have studied this in considerable detail when I had the privilege of representing India, at the United Nations, both in Geneva and New York. I have also had access to people who were around when some of these decisions were taken. Earlier in my career, I read widely on this issue. I saw no reason then and fail to see one now as to why such a reference was made. It could only have been made if one had an abiding faith in the manner in which the permanent members of the Security Council would react. Permanent members at that time were the same five members of today, and I think it was a case of misplaced faith. India did not realise that the Security Council was a one-way door. India, at that point of time, was a newly independent country and perhaps allowed its foreign and security policy to be largely directed from elsewhere. But it is not ideally the kind of decision that one takes because it has long term ramifications.

The second example is India's unsuccessful bid seeking membership to the Organisation of Islamic Cooperation (IOC) in the 1970s. It is not a decision that a government should take unless it has done its homework. The third is the period which was seemingly characterised by diplomacy of a higher order, when the Rajiv Gandhi government set up a summit level group of developing countries in September 1989, following the Ninth Non-aligned Meeting in Belgrade. India was partnering with countries like Egypt, Yugoslavia and Columbia and wanted to form a group of developing countries, to better negotiate with the developed world. It was called the Group of 15 or G-15. The underlying message was that if the countries of the global south would try and coalesce, they would be able to get their opinion across. Thus, even as late as 1989, India allowed its diplomacy to be guided by the need to make common cause. This stands in stark contrast to the present initiatives by Prime Minister Modi, where he has established a personal chemistry with world leaders. India has evidently evolved a great deal, but back then was still struggling in between the multilateral system, still in its old 1945 form. Indian presence is, however, still not always evident in much of the substantive and normative work that is being done in the multilateral system. Our missions remain understaffed, and are not able to produce and spare enough people to participate in the norm setting that is taking place and which will determine the contours of the world as it is going to evolve.

India missed the first industrial revolution because it was a colony. Today, it stands at the cusp of the fourth industrial revolution, which is all about delivering urban services and rebuilding India using instruments such as artificial intelligence, robotics, machine learning and the latest advancement technology has to offer. The country needs to make and build 700-900 million square meters of space between now and 2030 as part of its developmental effort. This means building one Chicago every year. Seventy per cent of the India of 2030 still remains to be built. This is the hard reality.

The multilateral system, as presently constituted, may perhaps not survive for long. The Security Council seems to have lost its credibility in the way it is operating, as seen by the number of major conflicts in the world. Yet, It remains the only agency in the world which can make a determination on whether there exists a threat to international peace and security and after making such determination, it is the only agency which can authorise the imposition of counter-measures. Yet, we see conflicts around the world where the use of force has not been authorised by the Security Council, except perhaps in Libya, which too went horribly wrong. There is tension in Syria, Yemen, Ukraine and in North Korea, where the Security Council is being completely ignored. There is thus a need for a different architecture, and it is important that India be a part of the design of that architecture, so that it is in a position to shape the outcome.

India is a player in the multilateral system, and it would be difficult for major interventions on issues such as climate change and trade to take place without India being on board. As of now, India is consulted at the last moment, but it would be better to engage in shaping the agenda right from the inception stage itself. The language that we speak and the work that we do, show and reveal the biases of the worldview that we have.

The size of the Indian economy which stands at USD 2.5 trillion and its rate of growth at 7-8 per cent, makes India an important player in world affairs. Soon, the Indian economy will be a USD 5-6 trillion economy and the per capita income will also be in the range of 5-6000 USD. This will put India in the top 3-5 countries, which makes it essential for India to have a say in the policies which shape the world. India is too important a country not to be on the main table in the Security Council. India is also far too important for global trade not to be participating in the processes at the level. Hence, it is time that India demands a central seat on all multilateral systems including the financial and trade institutions and ensure that its voice is heard and its concerns are addressed.

# 36

# The High Moral Ground

*Kanwal Sibal*

We are all very familiar with the long standing criticism of India's foreign policy being too moralistic and idealistic and often hear that India is not a practitioner of hard power. Many feel that this has been the bane of our foreign policy. I don't agree with this assumption. When a country follows a particular course in foreign policy, it is a reflection of the state of affairs globally and the internal dynamics in the country. The context in which these positions are taken in the international arena is important to consider as contexts keep changing and foreign policy keeps evolving. The earlier criticism of India continually assuming a moral high ground was a product of the circumstances of those times, both external and internal.

This attitude was also a product of Indian civilisation. There are not many countries in the world that have India's civilisational depth, and so India's position is oft based on centuries of ingrained values, on the way we look at life, at society and at the external world. Hence, the positions that India takes are based on the roots of her philosophical thinking, which encompass tolerance and acceptance of diversity. And it is this philosophy that views the world as one family and goes beyond a binary construct. India has also, always separated faith from politics and its outlook is genuinely secular. Hence, when India pronounces on foreign policy issues, it can hardly be expected to change its mindset and intrinsic worldview, when her innate ways of thinking and reflection take a totally different view.

It is this view that has been reflected in India's foreign policy and explains why India repudiated the Cold War. The Cold War was based on binaries of good and evil, and the two power blocs which confronted each other, had a diametrically opposite view of the other. For India, the belief was that difference could be resolved through dialogues and conversations, and that peace could be the outcome.

Another factor which shaped India's foreign policy was the manner in which India's independence movement unfolded. The struggle for independence was fought on moral grounds, moral values and moral principles. Mahatma Gandhi always averred that he was not against the British but was against British imperialism. The philosophy of his Satyagraha flowed from this belief and it was through negotiation that India obtained her independence. This explains why, at that time at the global level, India infused her foreign policy discourse with a high degree of moralism and moral content.

India was the first major country to gain independence from colonialism and therefore, within the UN system, it was India that led the campaign against colonialism. Later, India's campaign against apartheid was again rooted in moral values. India also took positions against nuclear weapons and was the prime mover of the Partial Test Ban Treaty. India was thus also in favour of disarmament and was against the Cold War. The policy of non-alignment was a product of this kind of a mindset, which was against dividing the world into opposing blocs.

While India has been criticised for adopting a moral high ground, etc., the entire structure that was built after the Second World War was based on moral values and all based on high moral ground. The UN has taken upon itself the mantle to save the world from the scourge of war. A cursory look at the Universal Declaration of Human Rights indicates that this declaration is based on moral values and principles. More than ever today, it is the US and Europe that have adopted a moral high ground and talked about moral values, which paradoxically is at variance with the actual actions on the ground. But the whole structure that they have built and the outlook that they disseminate and want others to accept is based on such kind of moral thought.

The crusade for democracy continues today. India has moved away from adopting moral high postures but progressively, such posturing is emanating from the Western countries led by the United States. Increasingly, the talk is about democracy and the will of the people, the responsibility to protect, human rights, freedom of expression, etc. The US has been in the forefront in negotiations pertaining to a wide range of international treaties, but despite that has stayed out of them, fearing that such treaties would curtail their freedom of action. Whether it is the International Court of Justice or the CTBT negotiations or even the United Nations Convention on the Law of the Seas, all of which the US negotiated but stayed out fearing constraints on their freedom of action.

India has always been a very strong supporter of multilateralism and opting out of the Cold War was in a way, a commitment to multilateralism. India's thrust on dialogue as a means to resolve differences through negotiation and her commitment to peaceful coexistence reflected a multilateral viewpoint. India seeks good relations with all countries and that is the basis of multilateralism. The Non-Aligned Movement itself was a product of this kind of thinking, which prompted India to play an active role in the UN and explains India's refusal to join any military blocs. This also explains India's proactive participation in the UN in various ways and the leading role played in terms of participation in UN peacekeeping operations and its role in non-proliferation treaty negotiations. India did not join the NPT as it was structured in such a way that it was discriminatory which India would not accept. Similarly, India participated in the CTBT negotiations, but again the treaty was steered in a way that it became a means to perpetuate the nuclear status of certain countries and deprive others permanently.

India is also a part of GATT, WTO and G20. Other multilateral organisations of which India is a part include all the UN financial organisations with the World Bank, IMF and the part of UNESCO. India is active in UNESCO, is a dialogue partner with ASEAN and is part of the ADMM-Plus (ASEAN Defence Ministers Meeting), which is a platform for ASEAN and its eight dialogue partners to strengthen security and defence co-operation for peace, stability, and development in the region. India is also part of the East Asian Summit and Climate Change negotiations. India is also deeply concerned on the whole issue of terrorism and counter-terrorism and has built up multilateral relations with many countries to focus world attention on this menace to the international community.

India is a member of BRICS and the SCO, which enables it to contribute multilaterally to platforms that address global issues. Many of these organisations comprise countries which are otherwise strategic adversaries of each other, but that has not deterred India, which now has carved out sufficient space for itself to be able to act on all these platforms. But the talk about high moral ground and high table really refers to a permanent membership of the UN Security Council, because short of that, India is already, in its own way, on the High Table everywhere, whether the forums be economic, political or security.

For some years now, India has openly claimed right to be a permanent member. There are some who think that India ought not to go around begging for permanent membership and that this will come about when India is stronger economically and when the world recognises that it cannot do without India. India has teamed up with Germany, Japan and Brazil as a group of four in trying to mobiliseits case for our permanent membership to the UN Security Council. In terms of various attributes however, such as demography, physical size, civilisational depth, potential of economic and military power and the independence of India's foreign policy thinking and the strategic autonomy that it needs to keep, India perhaps stands in a unique position and is uniquely placed and is incomparable to the others. Nevertheless, the fact remains that others too are claimants for permanent membership to the UN Security Council and so India is not unique in that regard.

Today, it is commonplace to hear that the world is no longer unipolar, but is becoming a multipolar world. It is a poly centric world in the making and in that construct, India is a pole and is so regarded by many of the world's major powers. It would be inconceivable to think of climate change negotiations reaching a worthwhile conclusion without India as a partner. The initiative that has been taken by Prime Minister Modi to set up the International Solar Alliance is again another facet of our multilateralism. But multilateralism today is under attack especially from the US, which has taken some steps to reduce their budgetary support for the UN and has even questioned the utility of the World body, calling it a mere talk shop. Some of the public statements emanating from the US have been rather brutal. Statements such as, "We are willing to work within the United Nations if we can, but we will work outside the United Nations if we must" are a pointer. Most of what the US is doing at the global level is without any UN remit. It is outside the UN Security Council and this is true of all of Europe too. When President Trump says, "America First," it does not show any great commitment to multilateralism or to the UN system per se, whether it be political or economic. India however unequivocally supports multilateralism, despite the fact that within the multilateral system, India has not had due recognition and her experience of the UN Security Council has been very negative.

Generally speaking, India has been kept out of many of the critical multilateral organisations, such as the Nuclear Suppliers Group, the MTCR (Missile Technology Control Regime) or the Australia Group. A lot of pressure has also been placed on India to join the Non-Proliferation Treaty. India has been subjected to sanctions for decades as part of multilateral structures established by the United States outside the UN system and through manipulation of the UN system, which have been inimical to India's interests. Even now, in the UN Security Council, China is protecting Masood Azhar and protecting Pakistan, notwithstanding Azhar's terrorist affiliations.

While India remains a firm supporter of the UN system, it has had a very negative experience with it which puts India in a dilemma. However, on balance, India views the UN system, despite its frailties and deficiencies, better to work with from the inside rather than from outside it. India therefore continues to oppose unilateralism and all attacks on the sovereignty of countries and military intervention in countries on the basis of promoting democracy or whatever else.

Today, as a result of political developments in India and the strong central leadership which has a clear vision of where they want to take India, India's reputation and stature has progressively gone up. India aims to create a body of countries which would back and support India in its thinking, views and aspirations. The aim remains to participate in the international system and build up support amongst a certain set of countries by being constructive, even when the issues are difficult. India's role in the Climate Change negotiations are an example of such constructive engagement.

We also see Britain knocking at India's doors, asking India to take a leadership role in the Commonwealth, and making some very attractive propositions to make sure that we get a proper formalised institutional role. The whole concept of the Indo-Pacific is also increasing the relevance and centrality of India in terms of security of the Indian Ocean and the Pacific Ocean. And if India's economy continues to grow at 7-8 or plus per cent and the country is able to achieve its targets in terms of the size of the economy, that will automatically open up many more doors than there are at present. Today, China is a prominent member of the Security Council but until a few years ago, within the UN Security Council, China kept a low profile. They built up their country and now, having done so very successfully, their ambitions and aspirations have grown and they have the means which enable them to talk of initiatives such as the Belt and Road Initiative. It is through economic and military strength that a country is enabled to exercise various foreign policy options and play on the international stage, with the opportunities that open up and expand immensely. This remains India's aim and it is towards this end that India is focussed on and towards which it is headed.

# List of Contributors

**Smt Sushma Swaraj** is the Minister of External Affairs, Government of India, since 26 May 2014. A leader of Bharatiya Janata Party, Ms Swaraj is the second woman to be India's Minister of External Affairs, after Indira Gandhi. She has been elected seven times as a Member of Parliament and three times as a Member of the Legislative Assembly.

**Shri M.J. Akbar** is a distinguished writer who has authored several internationally acclaimed books, mainly on the Indian subcontinent's complex history and the turbulent interaction between faith and definitions of nationalism. Shri M.J. Akbar has also had an illustrious career as a journalist and editor. He has served as Minister of State for External Affairs, Government of India and is a Rajya Sabha Member of Parliament.

**Shri Shakti Sinha** is a 1979 batch AGMUT cadre IAS officer. He has served as private secretary to India's former Prime Minister, Shri Atal Bihari Vajpayee, senior adviser to the Executive Director at the World Bank and in UN mission to Afghanistan. He was Chief Secretary of Andaman and Nicobar Islands, and then CMD of Delhi Transco Limited. He is presently, Director, Nehru Memorial Museum and Library.

**Shri Ram Madhav Varanasi** has been the Member of the National Executive and in charge of the media and public relations of the Rashtriya Swayamsevak Sangh. Presently, he is the National General Secretary of the Bharatiya Janata Party (BJP) and is Member, Board of Governor's, India Foundation.

**Capt Alok Bansal (IN)** is Director, India Foundation and Executive Director, South Asian Institute for Strategic Affairs (SAISA). He has been the Executive Director of the National Maritime Foundation (NMF) and has worked with the Institute of Defence Studies and Analyses (IDSA) and Centre for Land Warfare Studies (CLAWS) earlier. He has authored a book titled *Balochistan* *in Turmoil: Pakistan at Cross Roads* in 2009 and has co-edited several other books.

**Vice Admiral Shekhar Sinha (IN)**, after a distinguished career in the Indian Navy, retired as the FOC-in-C Western Naval Command. He is a recipient of the Param Vishisht Seva Medal (PVSM), Ati Vishisht Seva Medal (AVSM), and Nao Sena Medal (NM). Earlier in his career, he had commanded INS Hansa, INS Saryu, INS Shakti and INS Delhi. Presently, he is Member, Board of Trustees, India Foundation.

**Shri Alok Joshi** was formerly chief of Research and Analysis Wing (R&AW). Hailing from Lucknow, he graduated from Jawaharlal Nehru University, (JNU) where he completed his post-graduation in political science before joining the Indian Police Service (IPS), Haryana cadre in 1976. He is presently Chairman, National Technical Research Organisation (NTRO).

**Shri R.N. Ravi** is a 1976-batch Indian Police Service officer from Kerala. He has served as the Special Director of IB. Presently, he is Chairman, Joint Intelligence Committee, Government of India. The post has recently been re-designated as Deputy National Security Advisor (Internal Affairs).

**Dr. Subrahmanyam Jaishankar** is an Indian diplomat who served as Foreign Secretary of India from January 2015-January 2018. He joined Indian Foreign Service in 1977. He had previously served as Indian Ambassador to the United States (2013–2015), China (2009–2013) and the Czech Republic (2001–04), and as High Commissioner to Singapore (2007–09). Jaishankar also played a key role in negotiating the Indo-US civilian nuclear agreement.

**Gen. V.K. Singh** is the Minister of State for External Affairs, Government of India. He has previously served as the Chief of Army Staff of the Indian Army from 2010-2012. He was also awarded Yudh Seva Medal for operations as part of IPKF in Sri Lanka, the Ati Vishisht Seva Medal (AVSM) for distinguished service while commanding a counter-insurgency force in 2005 and Param Vishisht Seva Medal in recognition of his exceptional and distinguished services in the Eastern Theatre in 2009.

**Shri Suresh Prabhakar Prabhu** is the current Minister of Commerce & Industry, Government of India. He is qualified as an Indian Chartered Accountant & member of the Institute of Chartered Accountants of India. He was, during the Premiership of Atal Bihari Vajpayee of 1998 to 2004, Minister of Industry,

Minister of Environment and Forests; Fertilisers & Chemicals; Power; Heavy Industry and Public Enterprises.

**Shri Shaurya Doval** is the Managing Director of Zeus Caps, where he leads the principal investment initiatives and deal originations in India. Mr. Doval is a qualified Chartered Accountant and holds a joint MBA Degree from London Business School and University of Chicago. He is Member, Board of Governors, India Foundation.

**Shri David Frawley** is an American Hindu acharya and author, who has written more than thirty books on topics such as the Vedas, Hinduism, Yoga, Ayurveda and Vedic astrology. He is the founder and director of the American Institute of Vedic Studies in Santa Fe, New Mexico. He was awarded the Padma Bhushan in 2015.

**Shri Vinay Sahasrabuddhe** is an Indian politician & Member of Parliament of India representing state of Maharashtra in the Rajya Sabha. He was appointed as the President of Indian Council of Cultural Relations (ICCR), New Delhi in December 2017. He is also serving as National Vice President of Bharatiya Janata Party.

**Smt Veena Sikri** is Convener, South Asia Women's Network (SWAN) and Vice Chairperson, South Asia Foundation (SAF-India). She has served as the High Commissioner of India to Bangladesh and Malaysia & as the Consul General of India, Hong Kong. She has also served as the Head of Chancery, Embassy of India, Kathmandu (Nepal) and First Secretary, Permanent Mission of India to the UN, New York.

**Shri Vijay Chauthaiwale** holds a doctorate in microbiology. He is currently serving as the In-charge—Foreign Affairs Department, Bharatiya Janata Party.

**Shri Dhyaneshwar Mulay** is presently serving as Secretary, (CPV&OIA). He joined the Indian Foreign Service in 1983 and has served in Indian Missions in Tokyo, Moscow and Port Louis. He served as Minister in Damascus and was India's longest serving High Commissioner to Male.

**Shri Amar Sinha** retired from the Indian Foreign Service (IFS) as Secretary Economic Relations in the Ministry of External Affairs, New Delhi, in June 2017 after a diplomatic career spanning 35 years. He has served in different capacities in India missions around the world including in Algiers, Buenos

Aires, Washington DC, Jakarta and Brussels. He is a Distinguished Fellow at RIS (Research and Information System for Developing Countries) since November 2017.

**Shri Sanjaya Baru** is apolitical commentator and policy analyst, who has served as Secretary General, FICCI, India, until his resignation in April 2018. Dr. Baru has been Media Advisor to Prime Minister Manmohan Singh and Director for Geo-economics and Strategy, International Institute of Strategic Studies, London. Previously, he served as associate editor at The Economic Times and The Times of India, and then chief editor at Business Standard.

**Shri Vivek Katju** joined the Indian Foreign Service in 1975. He has served as India's ambassador to Afghanistan, Myanmar and Thailand and served in Indian Missions in Cairo, Abu Dhabi, Washington DC, Suva, and Kuala Lumpur.

**Shri Ashok K. Kantha** is Director, Institute of Chinese Studies, Delhi since 31 March 2017. A career diplomat, he has served as India's ambassador to China and as Secretary East, Ministry of External Affairs, Government of India. He has specialised in Asian affairs, with a particular focus on China.

**Professor Harsh V. Pant** is a Distinguished Fellow and Head of ORF's Strategic Studies programme. He holds a joint appointment with the Department of Defence Studies and King's India Institute as Professor of International Relations. He is also a Non-Resident Fellow with the Wadhwani Chair in US-India Policy Studies at the Center for Strategic and International Studies, Washington, DC.

**Shri Rajiv Sikri** retired in 2006 as Secretary (East) in India's Ministry of External Affairs after 36 years of distinguished service. He has served as India's Ambassador to Kazakhstan, and headed the Departments dealing with West Europe as well as the Soviet Union and East Europe. He has served as Deputy Chief of Mission in Paris, Deputy Consul General and Commercial Consul in New York and as Political First Secretary in Kathmandu.

**Shri Jawed Ashraf** joined the Indian Foreign Service in 1991. He has served in Frankfurt and Berlin and has worked in the Americas Division of Ministry of External Affairs in New Delhi. Presently, he is serving as High Commissioner of India to Singapore.

**Shri Dhruva Jaishankar** is Fellow in Foreign Policy Studies at Brookings India in New Delhi and the Brookings Institution in Washington DC. He is also a

Non-Resident Fellow with the Lowy Institute in Australia. His research examines India's role in the international system and the effects of global developments on India's politics, economics, and society, with a particular focus on India's relations with the United States, the Indo-Pacific, and Europe.

**Shri Pradeep Rawat** is an Indian Foreign Service (IFS) officer of the 1990 batch. He has served as Joint Secretary in the Ministry of External Affairs (MEA) before taking up his current assignment in Jakarta as Ambassador of India to Indonesia.

**Shri Arun Singh** joined the Indian Foreign Service in 1979. He has served as the Indian Ambassador to the United States and prior to that as India's ambassador to France. He has also served as India's ambassador to Israel and as Joint Secretary, in the Ministry of External Affairs. He is now a senior fellow with the Asia program at the German Marshall Fund of the United States.

**Shri Ashok Malik** is currently serving as the Press Secretary to the President of India. A journalist with over 20 years of experience, he was, prior to his current appointment, Distinguished Fellow at the Observer Research Foundation.

**Dr. Dattesh Prabhu Parulekar** is the Spokesperson of BJP Foreign Policy Cell, India. He is working as a research director in Indian School of Strategic Studies, Goa and Visiting Faculty at Naval War College, INS Mandovi, Goa. He is also an advisory member of Academic Council, India Studies Program and State University of Rio de Janeiro, Brazil. He is a Secretary-General of United Nations Association of Goa and Vice President of Forum for Integrated National Security, Goa.

**Shri P.S. Raghavan** is a career diplomat who has served as Ambassador of India to Russia, Ireland and Czechoslovakia. He is presently, Convener National Security Advisory Board, Government of India.

**Shri Rahul Roy-Chaudhury** is Senior Fellow for South Asia and Head of the South Asia programme in International Institute of Strategic Studies (IISS) London. He previously served in the National Security Council Secretariat in the Prime Minister's Office in India and was a senior faculty member at the Institute for Defence Studies and Analyses, New Delhi.

**Shri Ranjan Mathai** is a 1974 batch Indian Foreign Service Officer. He has served as Foreign Secretary, Government of India from 1 August 2011 to 31

July 2013. He has also served as Indian High Commissioner to the UK, Israel and Qatar.

**Shri Virendra Gupta** retired in 2016 after completing 37 years with the Indian Foreign Service. He served as India's High Commissioner in Tanzania, Trinidad & Tobago and South Africa. He has also served as Deputy Director General, IDSA (Institute for Defence Studies and Analyses).

**Dr. Martin Ney** is the German Ambassador to India since July 2015. From July 2012 until recently, he was the Legal Adviser of the German Foreign Office.

**Shri Hardeep Singh Puri** is Minister of State (IC) in the Ministry of Housing and Urban Affairs. He is a 1974 batch Indian Foreign Service officer who served as the Permanent Representative of India to the United Nations from 2009 to 2013. He has served as Chairman, United Nations Security Council Counter-Terrorism Committee, as Vice President, International Peace Institute and as Secretary-General, Independent Commission on Multilateralism in New York.

**Shri Kanwal Sibal** is an Indian Foreign Service Officer of the 1966 batch. He has served as India's Ambassador to Turkey, Egypt, France and Russia and after a distinguished career, retired as Foreign Secretary to the Government of India.

# Index